THE STORY
THAT SHAPES US

John H. Neufeld

THE STORY
THAT SHAPES US

Sermons
by
John H. Neufeld

CMBC Publications
Winnipeg, Manitoba
1997

CMBC Publications
600 Shaftesbury Blvd.
Winnipeg, Manitoba
R3P 0M4

We acknowledge, with thanks, a generous publishing subsidy from First Mennonite Church, Winnipeg, Manitoba

Cover: Gerald Loewen

Canadian Cataloguing in Publication Data

Neufeld, John H. (John Herman), 1933–

    The story that shapes us

    ISBN: 0-920718-56-6

1. Neufeld, John H. (John Herman), 1933– - Sermons. 2. Conference of Mennonites in Canada - Sermons. 3. Mennonites - Sermons. 4. Sermons, Canadian (English).* I. Title.

BX8127.N48 1997   252' .097   C97-920048-2

Printed in Canada by
Friesens
Altona, Manitoba
R0G 0B0

CONTENTS

Sexuality, Marriage and Family

Christian Living

FOREWORD

This book of sermons must be a near first for Canadian Mennonites. We know there are sermons of our predecessors hidden away in the archives. One can surmise that preachers, still living, have files full of them. Seldom have the sermons of a preacher, still fully alive, been collected and made available to a wider audience. One may presume that these sermons—stored, filed or published—have their own special story. Many were prayerfully birthed and carefully crafted. One can appreciate the many, sometimes agonizing hours, spent in study, reflection, writing and rewriting, in the creation of these "words strung together," as a sermon has been defined.

Even if one has the competency to craft a sermon, the delivery of it is another art. Humbly we admit, as Paul also claims, that we share "this treasure in jars of clay" (2 Corinthians 4:7 *NIV*). That is, the crafting of a sermon and its delivery are forms of self-disclosure. The message moves forward through our own humanity. Therefore, our preaching reveals the degree of our passion; it indicates our diligence or lack of it; it shows up our competences and weaknesses; it will reflect our love and our anger. Clearly the preacher becomes part of the text! Both, the creating and the preaching of a sermon, present onerous challenges for anyone in Christian ministry. Who is up to this challenge?

The author of this collection is an example of one who has an ongoing commitment to this arduous task. He is keenly aware that sharing the good news of Jesus Christ is the mandate entrusted to the church. Preaching is one of those ways. Gratefully we acknowledge that God, who blesses people with the competency to be ministers of the new covenant (2 Corinthains 3:5–6), also empowers for the task of preaching.

Those who accept the call to the ministry of preaching are commited to the Scriptures. In preparing a sermon they engage themselves with the text and its context. They are concerned about bringing the message of the Bible to their audience. In his preaching John Neufeld wants to convey to all of us that the Scriptures become relevant to life today.

We commend this collection of sermons to the reader. John, perhaps more than any other preacher in the constituency of the Conference of Mennonites in Canada, has given himself quite intentionally to the task of creating biblically based and relevant sermons. And, he has committed himself to teaching this art to his students and to all of us who have been privileged to hear him preach. We have been his students. The biblical injunction to "remember your leaders, who spoke the word of God to you . . ." (Hebrews 13:7) may apply also to those still living who generously and joyously share their gifts with the larger constituency.

Perhaps the only components missing in this collection of sermons are the voice, the tone, the emphasis, indeed the physical presence of the preacher, John H. Neufeld. That presence we need to imagine and create for ourselves as we read this treasure. Henry David Thoreau is right when he says. "It takes two to speak the truth—one to speak, and another to hear" (quoted in *Biblical Preaching,* Haddon W. Robinson, 23). In this collection the preacher is speaking, we the readers are hearing.

Menno H. Epp
Leamington, Ontario
March 1997

JOHN H. NEUFELD
THE MAKING OF A PREACHER

If you would have told John Neufeld forty-five years ago that a book of his sermons would be published, he never would have believed it. Being a preacher was the last thing he ever thought he would be in his life. Yet through some fortuitous circumstances, he found his way to the pulpit and the classroom and became an astute preacher and teacher.

John was born in 1933 and lived in Pigeon Lake, Manitoba, for the first few years of his life. He was the fourth child (although one brother had already passed away at a young age) of a family of five. He took his first year of school in Headingley, then lived in Springstein for the next four years where his father worked as farm manager for a local farmer. In 1945, John and his family moved to British Columbia in order to purchase their own farm. He attended Langley High School and took grade 12 and 13 at the Mennonite Educational Institute where he graduated in 1953. Following high school John hoped to pursue further studies at the University of British Columbia (UBC) in the area of science. Aptitude tests had confirmed that this is where he should be. Unfortunately—or perhaps fortunately—John couldn't earn enough money to afford going to university. In retrospect, it appeared that God had put a block in his way. Around the time he was making decisions about his future, a quartet from Canadian Mennonite Bible College (CMBC) was touring in the area and promoting the school. John decided he would go to CMBC for six months, then pursue studies toward a science degree. It was clear to him that he never wanted to be a preacher or a teacher. He describes himself as having been very uptight and apprehensive when it came to speaking in front of groups of people. To do public speaking distressed him.

Nonetheless, after his first semester at CMBC, John was there to stay. He enjoyed biblical studies, theology and Anabaptist-Mennonite history. He also happened to have a rather significant girlfriend, Anne Hiebert from Waldheim, Saskatchewan, who helped to keep him at the College. On June 24, 1955, John and Anne married in Waldeim. A year later their first child, Donna, was born in Winnipeg.

After graduating from CMBC John and Anne returned to BC. John entered UBC, not in the faculty of science but to get a teaching certificate. After a year of study, he began to teach in an elementary school. Needless to say, his fear of public speaking caught up with him, and the two years he taught children were filled with anxiety, even though children at the time were quite respectful of their teachers. After his second year of teaching John was encouraged to take a teaching position at Bethel Bible Institute (BBI), at that time the General Conference Bible Institute which later joined the Mennonite Brethren Bible School to form Columbia Bible Institute. John accepted the position with some reluctance and taught in the area of Christian Education. To his surprise, he was now much more relaxed about teaching and speaking in front of people generally. Why the change? Even before he left for CMBC, John had a Sunday school teacher whom he credits with helping him overcome his fear of speaking in front of people his own age. This teacher, Jake Baerg, encouraged students in a youth Sunday school class to teach each other the lesson. The practical experience helped John gain confidence in speaking to his peers, something that he lacked in teaching younger children. At BBI he taught young people—students close to his own age—how to teach children. This seemed like a more natural teaching role than he had before.

In 1959, after two years of teaching at BBI, the Commission on Overseas Missions (COM) invited John and Anne and their two preschoolers (Donna and Ken, born in 1958) to move to Uruguay for 16 months where John taught at the Mennonite Biblical Seminary in Montevideo. It was their COM assignment which prompted John's ordination. He had been working as an unpaid youth leader at Bethel Mennonite Church in Aldergrove and had preached there on occasion, yet up until then had never really faced a call to ministry. His ordination served as a backdrop to his mission assignment in Uruguay, a logical step, given the work he was to do. During this time he began to consider attending seminary and exploring ministry in a more intentional way.

After returning from Uruguay in 1961, John's plan was to do what he needed to do to prepare for going to seminary. He enrolled at Western Washington State College in Bellingham and completed his Bachelor of Arts in 1963. By now, John and Anne's family was again growing with the birth of Karen, their third child. For the next three years John continued to teach at BBI. In summers, he moved his family to Camp Squeah and worked as a camp director.

Finally in 1966, John and Anne had saved enough money to move to Elkhart, Indiana, so John could study at Mennonite Biblical Seminary.

Upon applying to Seminary, John requested information on employment opportunities in Elkhart. The president, Erland Waltner, arranged for him to take a pastoral position in an Evangelical United Brethren (Methodist) congregation. This was John's first pastoral ministry position. On a Thursday in the middle of June 1966, John, Anne and their children arrived in Elkhart with their belongings. By Sunday morning John was preaching in the church and did so every Sunday for the next three years (with the exception of only four Sundays) while he studied at Seminary. He also led weekly Bible studies and performed the usual weddings and funerals required of him.

John's experience in the Methodist church was significant. The congregation encouraged him to remain faithful to his Mennonite roots and identity, not expecting him to baptize infants and encouraging him to preach about peace and pacifism, even though the church had members who were active in the military. In his ministry to the Methodist church John began more fully to understand his own Mennonite faith and theology. He appreciated how openly the congregation affirmed and accepted him—a kind of affirmation he had not experienced in the Mennonite church.

While studying at Seminary John began to discover the Old Testament in a way he had not experienced before; this in turn influenced his preaching. The Old Testament allowed him to explore a narrative style of preaching as an alternative to the more traditional Mennonite sermons of "admonition." He appreciated the practical bent of the Old Testament stories, stories which could easily connect with the lives of those in his congregation. While at Seminary John became concerned with how the Bible was used in preaching. His course work in hermeneutics and biblical studies helped him to understand that to preach a good sermon meant using the Bible with integrity.

In his last year of studies, Waldemar Janzen, a professor from CMBC and member at First Mennonite Church in Winnipeg, visited the Seminary and told him of a pastoral opening at First Mennonite. At that time John and Anne were exploring options for the future. By now their fourth and last child, Brenda, had been born, and they were interested in finding a place where Anne could study and the four children could take music lessons. They were positively inclined toward moving to Winnipeg and, after entering a discerning process with the church, John accepted a position as associate pastor in 1969. Later in 1970, he was ordained a second time, this time as *Ältester;* in 1973 he became senior pastor of the church.

During his years at First Mennonite Church John was able to develop his gift of preaching. His pastoral involvement with parishioners deeply influenced his sermonizing. Visiting the sick and the dying, helping families deal with crises, teaching catechism classes to the youth, all helped him to realize the importance of not just exegeting a biblical text but also learning to exegete the lives of those to whom he was ministering. His experiences in church and his own life began to enter into his sermons more frequently, allowing the listeners to identify or contrast their lives with his. This, together with his commitment to sound biblical exegesis, gave his sermons depth and drew listeners in. Given this experience with preaching it is not surprising that later, in pursuing his Doctorate of Ministry at Bethany Theological Seminary in Oakbrook, Illinois, he focused on the place of preaching within the total ministry of the church. Through his experience John became very aware of the formative and cumulative impact that preaching had on the church. For many parishioners, the sermon was the only place where they could be involved in theological reflection. John took this realization very seriously as he carefully prepared his sermons, engaging in an exegesis both of the biblical text and of life.

First Mennonite gave John much freedom in developing his preaching gift. While a pastor there, he tackled a number of very difficult issues that were often not preached about. Wealth, divorce, family life issues, death and dying, conversion were all topics which John preached on, sometimes at his own risk. In First Mennonite Church he was free to work with new ideas. There was a sense of openness to test some biblical questions—questions raised by biblical scholarship and issues of interpretation. Parishioners encouraged John to include background information to particular biblical passages and soon grew to expect a context to be given for a text on which he preached.

In 1984 John was invited to accept the position of president at CMBC. This was a new and challenging role for him. Although he missed the richness of his involvement with senior citizens and the engagement with persons in a variety of life stages and experiences, he entered his new role with vigour. In his job as president John developed relationships with many congregations and pastors through the Conference of Mennonites in Canada. Through his administrative style, he developed a sense of collegiality with faculty and staff. He particularly enjoyed the students and they, in turn, found him approachable. Singing in chapel, teaching again in the classroom, interacting in the hallways and in his office—all were enriching experiences for John.

Yet his role as president was never an easy one. He describes his coming to CMBC in the fall of 1984 as "jumping on to a moving train that didn't stop when I got on board." He had to learn to live with the momentum of college life. Fundraising during difficult financial times, dealing with constituency suspicions and criticisms, working with an academic-minded faculty which was not very open in either its affirmation or its critiques, all presented challenges to John. Yet there was never a time when he dreaded going to work.

After functioning in his role for a year, John proposed to the faculty that they begin a preaching class. In 1986, a class was started with John as teacher. His many years of preaching experience together with a Doctorate of Ministry in the same field made him an excellent "teacher of preachers." The preaching course took off and has been part of CMBC's curriculum every year since. The essence of John's preaching classes has really been the essence of his own preaching success: serious engagement with the biblical text together with serious engagement with life. While some professors of homiletics focus primarily on either rhetoric or exegesis of the text, John has been interested in both content and communication and brought these together effectively in the classroom.

His students have consistently praised John as a teacher and preacher. The things which made him a good preacher, continue to make him a good teacher: his systematic pedagogy, his ability to ask the right questions, his keen power of observation and his ability to speak clearly and simply on complex issues. Simply put, John has a way with words. Students claim that in his sermons he knows how to "turn a phrase." He will long be remembered for phrases such as "a people with a bias" referring to the CMBC community and the larger Christian community, or "singing at midnight" referring to Paul and Silas in prison (Acts 16:25), a phrase which rings of faith and hope amidst strife.

Preacher, teacher, administrator . . . John's gifts have led him to places he never imagined he would be. It has been his life's work to help build bridges: between the Bible and the contemporary church, between academics and the laity, between theology and life experience, between CMBC and its constituency. To this end, he has served the church faithfully and with integrity.

Irma Fast Dueck
Winnipeg, Manitoba
March 1997

Stewardship
of the
Gospel

1

FROM CONFUSION TO CLARITY

Saul, still breathing threats and murder against the disciples of the Lord, went to the high priest and asked him for letters to the synagogues at Damascus, so that if he found any belonging to the Way, men or women, he might bring them bound to Jerusalem. Now as he was going along and approaching Damascus, suddenly a light from heaven flashed about him. He fell to the ground and heard a voice saying to him, "Saul, Saul, why do you persecute me?" He asked, "Who are you, Lord?" The reply came, " I am Jesus, whom you are persecuting. But get up and enter the city, and you will be told what you are to do." The men who were travelling with him stood speechless, because they heard the voice but saw no one. Saul got up from the ground, and though his eyes were open, he could see nothing; so they led him by the hand and brought him into Damascus. For three days he was without sight, and neither ate nor drank (Acts 9:1–9).

I am reminded of your sincere faith, a faith that lived first in your grandmother Lois and your mother Eunice and now, I am sure, lives in you. For this reason I remind you to rekindle the gift of God that is within you through the laying on of my hands; for God did not give us a spirit of cowardice, but a spirit of power and of love and of self-discipline. . . . But as for you, continue in what you have learned and firmly believed, knowing from whom you learned it, and how from childhood you have known the sacred writings that are able to instruct you for salvation through faith in Christ Jesus (2 Timothy 1:5–7, 3:14–15).

Many people in the church have questions about the experience of conversion. For many it is a personal, existential question: "How can I be sure that I am converted? Is there a right way to experience conversion?" In some circles, expressions like "born again," "saved" are frequently used; in others we hear about "belief" and "commitment."

First preached in March 1986 at First Mennonite Church, Winnipeg, Manitoba.

Does it matter which words or phrases we use?

Some years ago a relative of mine heard me preach at First Menno-nite Church. Over lunch he said, "But John, you didn't preach the gospel."

"What do you mean?" I asked.

"Well, you didn't mention 'the blood' once."

I thought I had preached the gospel. He didn't. Were we both hooked on language—and judging the other on whether he did or did not use the right "code" words? What should we expect when we meet with a group of baptismal candidates? How can we tell if they are really ready for baptism? Will the experience of someone raised in a Christian home be different than that of someone raised without Christian nurture?

I hope these two sermons (see also Sermon 2 below: "From Inno-cence to Owned Faith") on conversion will give some clarity on these and other questions. I hope that each of you will come to a clearer understanding of your own conversion and commitment to Christ, or that you will feel led to make a decision. I hope that through these sermons some may decide to become Christians, and that all who are already believers will be renewed in their faith.

When I think of conversion I cannot but remember my own experience. I grew up in the Fraser Valley of British Columbia and for two years attended Mennonite Educational Institute in Clearbrook. Fridays were the days on which testimonials were given. Some of my classmates told of their precise, datable experiences of being converted; I could not. I came to doubt my own experience because I couldn't get any closer than to say I'd made a decision during a certain winter. In the face of my friends' precise accounts I doubted whether I even was a Christian.

Paul and Timothy. Imagine you are in an audience hearing an interview with Paul and Timothy. It's being taped for airing on the CBC television program "Man Alive." Roy Bonisteel, the host, has been talking to both of them, reviewing their biographical data and their most recent experiences.

Then, "Paul, I've been meaning to ask you: How did you become a Christian? I understand it was well into your adult years when you made a dramatic switch. I'm actually surprised that you, a person strongly committed in one direction, made such an about-face."

To this Paul replies, "Yes, I remember it as though it were yesterday, and it's been years already. I was on my way to Damascus to round up Christians for the Sanhedrin. I remember carrying the authorization papers for my mission of arresting others.

"On that road I myself was arrested by a penetrating question, 'Saul,

Saul, why do you persecute me?' I had heard my name, graciously repeated. The word 'persecute' brought back a stinging memory. I thought of stones hitting human flesh, and I heard again the prayer of Stephen asking for the forgiveness of those who threw the stones. I remembered consenting to that innocent man's death. Now the same Jesus to whom Stephen had prayed was confronting me.

"I had to be led to Damascus. There a Christian brother approached me with the words, 'Brother Saul.' At that moment I knew I had been reborn. I will never forget that day. Whenever I have doubts, I remember that experience and I know the unseen world is real. I was adopted by a new group. I began to work for Jesus."

Turning to Timothy, the interviewer asks, "Well, Timothy, I imagine you've had a similar experience."

"Well, no, actually I cannot give you a dramatic story like Paul's."

"But you are a Christian, aren't you?"

"Yes, I am. Let me explain. I grew up in a believing home. We were very much made aware of the presence of God. We were told of the sacred writing (2 Timothy 3:14). I remember my grandmother Lois and my mother Eunice each playing a vital role."

"But when did you become a Christian?"

"I find that hard to answer. I don't remember a day when I was converted. I accepted what I had been taught; I believed it firmly and began to live as one of the disciples of the Lord (Acts 16:1)."

Although these two experiences are very different, in several ways they are the same. Both Paul and Timothy came to acknowledge Jesus as Lord and Saviour and surrendered their lives to him. Both of them began to obey, to follow Jesus in life as best they could. For each of them faith was three things: knowing, trusting and doing. Both of them, in spite of their different experiences, were part of the church.

Three patterns. In his classic study, *The Varieties of Religious Experience,* William James writes: "To be converted . . . denotes the process, gradual or sudden, by which a self hitherto divided . . . becomes unified and consciously right." When I listen in on Paul and Timothy telling their stories and when I hear James commenting on the varieties of religious experience, and set that against my own experience, I feel somewhat disturbed. In my growing-up years and in recent years, I have heard about conversions like Paul's—sudden, climactic, emotional, datable, rememberable—but rarely has Timothy's gradual process beginning in childhood, a conscious but unemotional affirmation, been held high as a valid experience. In recent years when I have asked groups whether they had datable conversions or gradual ones, always both were represented. And persons whose experience were more like Timothy's breathed a sigh of relief that they were OK too.

Hans Kasdorf, a Mennonite Brethren scholar, has written that we need to affirm not only these two patterns, but also a third which he calls "peak experiences" (based on Abrahm Maslow's, *Religions, Values and Peak Experiences,* 1946). Kasdorf also gives three cases to illustrate each of them. With which do you identify?

Story 1: The conversion of a weaver in Brazil. I was standing close to a weaving machine, watching the intricate work of the instrument fashioning the warp and the woof until a sizable roll of fine cotton fabric was ready for release. The man on the chair was Adolf Stinshoff, owner of the factory in Blumenau, Brazil. The Stinshoffs were regular participants in our worship services and Bible study meetings in the church where I was pastor.

"So it was in my life," Mr. Stinshoff said, as we discussed the analogy between the work of the weaving machine and God's work in people's lives. "God is a Master Weaver. I grew up under the influence of godly parents," he continued as we walked to the house to join Mrs. Stinshoff for morning coffee. "God spun and weaved until I consciously was prepared to assume the role of discipleship."

"But how did you experience conversion?" I queried.

"Conversion? I don't know," he replied. Then he added, "I know when I was baptized, but I know neither time nor place of conversion. In fact, I don't even know of an experience which I can call my conversion to Christ. What I do know is that I am a child of God through Jesus Christ, my Lord, and I rejoice in his service."

Story 2: The conversion of a medic in Russia. "I had spent three years as a medic on the Turkish front during World War I. When I was released, I went back to my home in Russia.

"Although my parents gave me a comfortable bed and good food, I could neither sleep nor eat. The words of a dying soldier on the battlefield haunted me day and night, 'Kardash su wirasim' ('Brother, give me water'). Instead of giving him to drink, I deprived him of a wooden spoon and a piece of soap. My parents thought my problem was due to a love affair, but it was a guilty conscience.

"Then on a Sunday night, June 18th, God sent me a Sunday school teacher. This man had become burdened about my spiritual condition. He invited me to go for a walk. As we came to the forest, he revealed his purpose for coming and asked me whether I wanted to be converted. I responded affirmatively, but insisted that I could not be saved because of the great sin in my life, particularly the episode on the battlefield.

"My friend counselled with me, read various portions of scripture, and pointed to God's word in Isaiah 1:18: 'Though your sins are like scarlet, they shall be as white as snow; though they are red like crimson, they shall become like wool.'

"We knelt right there on the road. My friend prayed and asked me to pray too. I had no words; I could not pray. Then finally I cried to God. My heart was in agony. God forgave me. Now I felt relief. My burden was gone and I could thank God for forgiveness.

"As we got up from our knees, a group of young men approached us. God gave me courage to tell them of my conversion experience and to ask whether they wanted to be converted as well. Most of them disappeared, but two were converted. That resulted in a great revival in our village."

Story 3: The conversion of a psychiatrist in Japan. "When I was a medical student at the university, I had my first encounter with a Christian," related the Japanese psychiatrist, Dr. Tetsuo Kashiwagi, before an audience in a church in Fresno, California, on July 27, 1975. "My girlfriend invited me to Christian meetings," Kashiwagi continued. "The people there impressed me. They seemed to possess a sense of security and displayed a spirit of serenity which I liked, but lacked."

As the people listened to Kashiwagi's fascinating story and expected him to climax it by telling them of a sudden, cataclysmic conversion experience, the speaker said, "My conversion took five years during which I read the Bible, first sporadically, then more regularly. Each time I attended a Christian worship service or read the Bible, I experienced a change in my life; each experience was a kind of climax. Finally, I decided to be baptized. I asked the pastor to hold me down as long as possible. I stayed under water 80 seconds, my fiancée told me, and prayed for forgiveness of sins. When I stepped out of the water, I knew that I was a newborn man."

On the basis of scripture, personal experiences and psychological observations we can say that the experience of conversion is not uniform but diverse. We cannot standardize the experience, and we certainly cannot expect everyone else to have the same experience we had. We need to affirm, accept, rejoice in the great variety of conversions people have. The New Testament clearly states, "The Spirit blows where he wills."

2

FROM INNOCENCE TO OWNED FAITH

Hear, O Israel: The Lord is our God, the Lord alone. You shall love the Lord your God with all your heart, and with all your soul, and with all your might. Keep these words that I am commanding you today in your heart. Recite them to your children and talk about them when you are at home, and when you are away, when you lie down, and when you rise. Bind them as a sign on your hand, fix them as an emblem on your forehead, and write them on the doorposts of your house and on your gates (Deuteronomy 6:4–9).

But as for you, continue in what you have learned and firmly believed, knowing from whom you learned it, and how from childhood you have the sacred writings that are able to instruct you for salvation through faith in Christ Jesus (2 Timothy 3:14–15).

We live by story—by the stories we tell and hear and how those stories intersect with the story of God and God's people. We also live by words and by expectations.

We live by story. Remember the stories of Paul, Timothy, the Brazilian weaver, the Russian medic and the Japanese psychiatrist (see Sermon 1 above, "From Confusion to Clarity"). We saw ourselves in those stories. We were moved by them. Of course, anyone has the freedom not to believe; anyone has the freedom to refuse to see themselves in any of these stories. However, each of these five persons said yes to Jesus, became part of the church, Christ's body, and lived as a disciple.

We live by words. Think of the power of two words, "I do," spoken in a wedding service. Think of the power of the words, "I love you." Various professions have their languages: computers, medicine, football. Everyone who wants to "be in" has to learn the "in" language. Can you imagine working on computers or in medicine without learning the language? And the Christian faith has key words by which we

First preached in November 1989 at First Mennonite Church, Winnipeg, Manitoba.

live—and as Christians we must become familiar with them.

We could spend a good deal of time considering the words we use for Christian experience—born again, faith, saved, reconciled, redeemed, conversion—but that's not what this sermon is about. I want to emphasize one thing: just as there is a variety of legitimate religious experiences, there is also a range of words which are all OK.

What we want to look at more closely are expectations. When it comes to getting right with God and others, do we expect the same thing from those who grow up in a Christian family and in the church as from those who do not? Perhaps I can pose the issue by referring to Elizabeth Penner and Nicky Cruz. Will Elizabeth Penner, nurtured in a Bethel family and raised within the life of the congregation, experience salvation in a way similar to that of Nicky Cruz, who grew up in a street gang in New York City? The conversion of Nicky Cruz was a sensation, "a trophy catch," a gripping story. The story of Liz Penner will probably not be written up—it is so ordinary. Ordinary, yes, but also terribly important.

Think about these two a bit more. Is it to Liz's advantage that the family in which she grew up was Christian, that she attended Sunday school, learned to pray, went to church, youth group and camps? Does Liz's nurturing experience guarantee that she will be a Christian? Certainly not. Not a guarantee but certainly a privilege.

Yet as parents, do we not sometimes secretly wish that as our children grow up they could have a critical, decisive conversion experience? Haven't we sometimes wished that after a period of estrangement or alienation they would experience a real conversion? Then we would be *sure* that they had really responded to the call of Christ in their lives.

In 1983 Marlin Jeschke published a helpful book, *Believers Baptism for Children of the Church,* in which he argues that the gradual way of nurture through accountability is the more excellent way for those who have the advantage, the privilege, of Christian nurture. Jeschke argues that the New Testament pattern of conversion and baptism is that the adult convert enters the church from the outside world. He feels that this pattern will continue as long as the church is faithful in communicating the gospel so that persons from the non-Christian world continue to cross over into the Christian faith, both here in our society and anywhere in the world.

However, for us and our children the situation has changed. As Christian parents we have created a new environment for children so that they do not need to grow up in a non-Christian setting but, as Paul says, they can be brought up "in the discipline and instruction of the Lord" (Ephesians 6:2). Our children are within the nurturing experience as described in Deuteronomy, an environment which models by example and instructs by word of mouth, in both formal and informal settings, the meanings of the faith by which parents and the spiritual community live. This is an advantage and a privilege, but it does not remove the necessity of personal decision, of each person owning the faith. We hope that each of them will appreciate and appropriate the faith in which they have been nurtured. We cannot expect that they will have to reject, to repudiate their earlier way of life and embrace a new one. They should only have to affirm the faith and the community of faith in which they have grown up.

Before we consider how that might happen, we need to look at how we view children. What do we believe about children? According to some, the question is, "Are our children saved or lost?" Jeschke believes it is neither of these. Children are innocent, not responsible or account-able for their behaviour. If we believe this, we do not accept Roman Catholic teaching that children are guilty of original sin and need baptismal regeneration. If we believe that children are innocent, we also reject sixteenth-century Puritans who taught that children are "totally depraved and lost." We reject Jonathan Edwards' view (1740) that children are "young vipers, who are in the most miserable condition if they are out of Christ." We also reject the views of Dwight Moody, Ira Sankey and Charles Finney who believed that the child had to be lost before he/she could be saved. We also reject the teaching of John H. Oberholtzer (1935) that, "any child is already lost or soon will be."

According to the *Mennonite Encyclopedia* article, "Original Sin," our forefathers held that "innocent children are not accountable and are acceptable to God," and "so also Adam's sin does not impair anybody except the one who makes it a part of his own being." Prior to the age of accountability, they are not lost or responsible, nor are they able to make the response necessary for conversion in the New Testament sense (Gideon Yoder). E. Stanley Jones puts it this way, "Children are in the kingdom of God, and get out only by sinning out."

During childhood we must nurture them toward faith, inviting them to respond to God's love and call with child-faith. They are not capable of an adult faith. They respond as children to the story of Jesus; they invite him into their lives; they pray. We need to affirm and accept this level of response as appropriate to their being children.

To believe in the innocence of our children means that there comes a time of personal accountability, a time in which they become morally and spiritually responsible. Jeschke places this time during adolescence. He also believes it is possible to help youth move from innocence directly into faith.

We practice believers baptism—and this does not mean that someone has to be a big sinner before he/she is qualified to be saved. The only qualification for salvation is faith. When youth become aware of the alternatives, they stand before a genuine personal choice: not to choose the alternative of disobedience and alienation from God, but rather obedience and identification with God (Jeschke: 115). It is at this point that we use a term which had become widely used in recent years: owned faith. John Westerhoff who coined it calls it "a faith made their own following a stage of searching, reflection and self-conscious enquiry."

The *move* our young people make to owned faith is more difficult to discern than the switch of a convert from the non-Christian world into the realm of faith. Think of Elizabeth Penner and Nicky Cruz. But the signs of the owned faith will be there in both. The decision of faith by a youth of the church may not be expected to show the dramatic contrast of a converted adult. But the confession of faith will include conscious acceptance of Jesus as Lord and Saviour and a decision to walk in the way of Jesus (discipleship) in the company of others (the church).

"Do you believe in Jesus as the one who forgives your sin? Do you want to be his follower? Do you identify with his body, the church?" If so, then you ought to be baptized, be received into the church, and continue in the life of growth and discipleship.

This "owned faith" was part of Timothy's experience—not so much a crossing over from the non-Christian world into the sphere of the church, but rather a conscious appropriation of the faith in which he grew up. Not necessarily sensation, but still very important. The advantage of the path of nurture is that children and youth receive the sustained teaching of the faith and the modelling of the Christian life. The trap we may fall into is to believe that personal decision is no longer necessary. Personal, owned faith is not hereditary; it is not received somehow by osmosis; it must be personally held.

On a Sunday about ten years ago a group of baptismal candidates was introduced to the congregation. On Monday a grandfather was in my office. "How come our grandson wasn't on the list? He was in class; he's old enough. We hoped he'd take the step this year."

My response, "There's a very good reason he's not included. I talked with him last Thursday and he told me he didn't believe."

In our youth and membership classes we need to invite young people and adults to "declare" where they are at. In our families the first question cannot be, "Are you going to be baptized this year?" The first one is, "Do you believe? Are you willing to commit yourself to Christ, the church, discipleship?"

When we take this approach, we may experience pain and disappointment. Some will say, "Not yet," or " No way." That means they have consciously decided to live as non-Christians for the time being. As parents and churches we respect their decision (voluntarism) and suffer. When this happens, let us continue to relate, to love, to show care, to pray.

Remember that not everyone's timetable includes baptism at age 17 or 18. We trust that the Word planted in their lives through nurture will be watered by the Spirit, moulded by experiences and that, in due time, they will return. Some have returned at age 45, some at 61. When this happens, we also examine our Christian education program and our family life and determine where we may have fallen short. Maybe we have done so by our flawed example. Maybe not. Each one is a choosing person; there are other influences, invited and uninvited; there is the person's own will over which we have no control—not even God does. Jesus respected the "No" of a person. We must do all we can in a relaxed, unanxious way and invite people to respond according to their readiness, believing that the Lord is at work in each person's life.

I close with the words of Jeschke: "Let's face it, and gladly face it. The situation of children in the church *is* different. The more effective the job Christian parents and the church do of guiding their children into the Christian way, the less likely it is that these children and youth *can* have a dramatic conversion experience. . . . We must learn to exult in the . . . testimony of Christians . . . who joyfully embraced in adolescence and for all of their life thereafter the Christian way taught and modelled for them by the church" (Jeschke: 78).

3

MEMORIES AND QUESTIONS

As you therefore have received Christ Jesus the Lord, continue to live your lives in him, rooted and built up in him and established in the faith, just as you were taught, abounding in thanksgiving (Colossians 2:6–7).

The book, *Going to the Root* by Christian Smith, includes an insightful chapter on evangelism. Smith says that evangelism these days is tough. We make use of Christian jewellery, bumper stickers, padded pews, films and videos, yet people don't seem to be listening; we present a "weak, silly rendition of the gospel. The gospel of God's kingdom is indeed simple. But it is not just simple, it is also very deep." It is a demanding message which "calls us to become slaves to righteousness and justice, to lay down our lives, to take up our crosses, to put to death our old nature." We need something that cuts through the glitter. Underneath, "many people yearn, not for what is cheap and easy, but for what is meaningful—even if difficult and challenging" (Smith: 122–126).

Let's talk evangelism—a good word with a bad reputation; a good word which evokes and calls forth all sorts of memories and feelings which we might prefer not to awaken; a good word about "good news" which doesn't always taste so good. The word and the practice of evangelism have fallen on hard times for many people in my generation and for many in every generation.

When I started working on this topic, one of the things I did was stop a few people and ask them, "What is the first thing that comes to your mind when you hear the word evangelism?" I was saddened but not surprised by their responses: "Not good; count me out; I have little use for evangelism;" responses of cynicism and negativism. Were these persons out on the street, persons who were on the fringe of congregational life? No, they were persons in the centre of our churches, persons who have studied the Bible and are active church members. Why was

Presented in February 1993 at the annual sessions of the Conference of Mennonites in Manitoba.

the word evangelism so negative for them? What would your response have been? I mean your *real* response, not what you think a preacher wanted to hear, but what you really felt deep down, based on your own experiences or on the experiences that others have had.

This one word activates memories and emotions which we don't really want to face up to but know that we should. For some, evangelism brings up the image of the tent meeting—George Brunk's revival campaigns here in Manitoba and elsewhere; or a large crusade in an open air stadium—Billy Graham in Seattle in 1951—I was there; or evangelist A.G. Neufeld, with the booming voice, that imposing presence, those piercing eyes conducting evangelistic services in many of our churches and in Paraguay and Brazil; or the blind evangelist, Rev. Esau, who also spent time in my home when I was a teenager. We went to those services; we listened and we were moved. Some of us were converted under the ministry of these men. Others turned away, never to come back.

Every service included singing, preaching and an altar call with the singing of many verses of "Just as I am, without one plea." Some of our younger people have not experienced these things. Some of them have seen TV evangelists ranting and raving on the screen, roaming around their podiums Bible in hand, tears running down their cheeks, asking people to come forward.

Are these our dominant images of evangelism? Surveys show that only a small percentage of Christians, one half of one percent, come to faith via such crusades. The majority come by other ways, yet the dominant understanding of evangelism is shaped by the revival campaign and its resulting emotional aftermath.

For a few evangelism brings memories of caring friendship, open dialogue, warmth and joy, but for too many evangelism stirs the emotions: discomfort, guilt, pressure, fear, manipulation, disgust, exploitation, arm twisting, shallowness and superficiality. Do you find yourself identifying with any of these terms? The good ones or the not so good ones? I sense that we have a whole basketful of stuff in our collective memory bank.

I too have some negative memories of evangelism, but I have also come to the conclusion again that biblical evangelism is not an option for us, something that we can take or leave, according to our interest. It is something in which we must be engaged. It is part of being Christian. We cannot get around the biblical mandate to share the good news of the gospel with others.

We hear Paul say, "I beg you, be reconciled to God." That sounds to me like using words. We are called to do what Andrew did for Peter. He went to him with words of personal testimony, "We have found the Christ," and invited him to come and find out for himself. We also recall biblical images, calling all believers to be salt and light, to witness and evangelize, preach, make disciples. We know these things; we know we ought to do them. We read about the early church in Acts and our forebears in the 16th century, the Anabaptists, growing by leaps and bounds. We compare this to our own dismal record, and we realize once more that we've fallen far short of the Bible's expectations. Some feel guilty; some are paralyzed; some remind us to get back to the old ways.

Some respond to their past experiences with evangelism with a ready answer, even a theological one: "We're committed to discipleship and service and peace and justice—to the important stuff. We detest anything superficial." Others admit they have difficulty verbalizing their faith and are critical of the way others do it. "We prefer deeds to words." "We are allergic to cheap words" (Calvin Shenk). We are tempted to claim that everything we do is in fact evangelism. This may sound fine at first, but it isn't fine. It's probably no more than a half-truth. We must become more explicit about the foundations of our faith and our life.

I thought about these memories, my own and others; I thought about the biblical call to witness; I thought about the good word gone bad. Then I browsed through the New Testament. In my browsing I came across a statement in Paul which I don't recall noticing before, a most surprising statement, "We were gentle among you, like a nurse tenderly caring for her own children" (1 Thessalonians 2:7). That's how Paul describes his evangelistic-missionary work in Thessalonica. Amazing. Gentle as a nurse whose uppermost concern is for the patient, no pressure, no manipulation. Gentle as a nurse. Paul, the persecutor, become gentle as a nurse.

That would make a difference, wouldn't it? Would memories of negativism, fear and guilt, remain after experiencing a sharing of the gospel that was gentle as a nurse? What does this suggest for evangelism, our attitudes and our practices? What does this image suggest about how we approach people? Henri Nouwen writes, "Our task in evangelism is to clear away the weeds, to pull away the rocks, to allow the plants to grow." Here again, suggestions of tenderness, patience and gentleness. Paul's statement is a real challenge. Can we relate to sinners and seekers and our own mixed-up people—younger and older, and our children—in gospel-like ways? Caringly, lovingly, gently?

I have taken considerable time to name our memories regarding evangelism, to bring them to the surface so that we can begin to deal with them. And to suggest that Paul's statement in 1 Thessalonians 2:7 may be most helpful as a guideline as we think about being involved in evangelism in our time.

Of course there are other questions. You've had them racing around in your mind. For me another important question has to do with the amount of time it takes to make an important decision. I wondered about this analogy: how long does it take to choose a life's partner (or a faith)? Would we rejoice if our sons or daughters came home one day sharing that they had just met the most wonderful person in the world and that they wanted to be married in ten days? Would we rejoice with them or would we speak a word of caution? How long does it actually take to grow faith that lasts and has an abiding impact on our lives? I assume that when we share our faith we are not only interested in giving someone a life insurance policy for eternity. No, we are interested in much more than that: that they will enter into a process of transformation, that they will leave things behind, that they will change in their lives, and that they will begin to take the cues and directives for their lives from the Lord and his kingdom.

What does it take to grow the kind of faith commitment which is assumed as the basis of the words of Paul in Colossians 2:6–7? Receiving Christ Jesus as Lord is not an invitation to find a permanent parking spot but is actually a launch pad (Perry Yoder) which sends us on a pilgrimage to continue to live in him, rooted, built up, strengthened in the faith?

Let us recapture the meaning of the good word evangelism, to incarnate in our relationships with others that the good news of Jesus can be shared gently and invitingly. Let us help our churches to give up anti-gospel ways of sharing the gospel. Let us be biblical and holistic in our approach, recognizing that biblical evangelism—sharing the good news—includes personal faith in Jesus as Saviour and Lord and inclusion into the body of Christ, the believing community, and that it involves actively following Christ as disciples, serving the world as salt, light and witnesses.

4

"I WANT YOUR VINEYARD"

Naboth the Jezreelite had a vineyard in Jezreel, beside the palace of King Ahab of Samaria. And Ahab said to Naboth, "Give me your vineyard, so that I may have it for a vegetable garden, because it is near my house; I will give you a better vineyard for it; or, if it seems good to you, I will give you its value in money." But Naboth said to Ahab, "The Lord forbid that I should give you my ancestral inheritance." Ahab went home resentful and sullen because of what Naboth the Jezreelite had said to him; for he had said, "I will not give you my ancestral inheritance." He lay down on his bed, turned away his face, and would not eat.

His wife Jezebel came to him and said, "Why are you so depressed that you will not eat?" He said to her, "Because I spoke to Naboth the Jezreelite and said to him, 'Give me your vineyard for money; or else, if you prefer, I will give you another vineyard for it'; but he answered, 'I will not give you my vineyard.'" His wife Jezebel said to him, "Do you not govern Israel? Get up, eat some food, and be cheerful; I will give you the vineyard of Naboth the Jezreelite."

So she wrote letters in Ahab's name and sealed them with his seal; she sent the letters to the elders and the nobles who lived with Naboth in the city. She wrote in the letters, "Proclaim a fast, and seat Naboth at the head of the assembly; seat two scoundrels opposite him, and have them bring a charge against him, saying, 'You have cursed God and the king.' Then take him out, and stone him to death." The men of his city, the elders and the nobles who lived in his city, did as Jezebel had sent word to them. Just as it was written in the letters that she had sent to them, they proclaimed a fast and seated Naboth at the head of the assembly. The two scoundrels came in and sat opposite him; and the scoundrels brought a charge against Naboth, in the presence of the people, saying, "Naboth cursed God and the king." So they

First preached in November 1977 at First Mennonite Church, Winnipeg, Manitoba.

took him outside the city, and stoned him to death. Then they sent to Jezebel, saying, "Naboth has been stoned; he is dead."

As soon as Jezebel heard that Naboth had been stoned and was dead, Jezebel said to Ahab, "Go, take possession of the vineyard of Naboth the Jezreelite, which he refused to give you for money; for Naboth is not alive, but dead." As soon as Ahab heard that Naboth was dead, Ahab set out to go down to the vineyard of Naboth the Jezreelite, to take possession of it.

Then the word of the Lord came to Elijah the Tishbite, saying: Go down to meet King Ahab of Israel, who rules in Samaria; he is now in the vineyard of Naboth, where he has gone to take possession. You shall say to him, "Thus says the Lord: Have you killed, and also taken possession?" You shall say to him, "Thus says the Lord: In the place where dogs licked up the blood of Naboth, dogs will also lick up your blood" (1 Kings 21:1-19).

The story in 1 Kings 21 is a rather frightening one. It tells of one of the blackest crimes that ever blotted a page of history. Although the story comes from a time long past and a culture quite different than our own, it touches your life and mine. It matters little whether you are 17 or 70 or even seven, this story has something to say to each one of us. It is a mirror in which we will see something about ourselves, our time, our society—if we dare to take a look.

Come along with me then to Ahab's winter palace in Jezreel; let's see what's going on there. Our text gives none of the background to the incident. It simply states that next door to the king's property lay a piece of land owned by Naboth. He used his land to cultivate grapes on its terraced slopes.

One day Ahab went for a walk and met his neighbour Naboth outside in his vineyard. After the usual greetings Ahab said, "Say, Naboth, my friend, let me have your vineyard. It's close to my palace and I'd like to use it for a vegetable garden. I'll either get you another piece of property or I'll pay you in cash. Would you like to trade or sell?"

To Ahab's surprise, Naboth his peasant neighbour answered immediately and simply— he knew the laws and customs, that property was to be handed down through the family line, unless there were no heirs—the land was not to be sold.

Ahab knew Naboth's legal rights, that he wasn't really allowed to get rid of his property. So Ahab returned home sulking, depressed and angry. He went straight to his bedroom. He threw himself on his ivory trimmed bed and turned his face to the wall. The servants came in at meal time but he refused to eat. When word finally got to his wife Jezebel that the King was not eating anything they asked her, "What is wrong with the King, your husband. He won't eat?"

Like most wives she was concerned about her husband. She went to his room and asked, "Dear, why are you so depressed? Why won't you eat?"

"Oh it's nothing, Jezebel. I just offered our neighbour over there a trade or cash for his garden and he refused me. Right away. So I'm mad. He told me I couldn't have his vineyard but I wanted it so badly."

When Jezebel heard what had happened, the "wheels started turning" and she had a scheme ready in a matter of minutes. "Imagine that, Ahab. Are you the King or aren't you? Get out of bed, eat your supper, cheer up. I'll get you that vineyard." What did she do? She wrote letters on the palace stationery, and signed with the King's official seal, then arranged for a couple of village scoundrels to get up at the community meeting and accuse Naboth of blasphemy and insubordination to the King. All went according to her plan and Naboth was convicted and stoned to death.

When Jezebel got the message that it was all done, she paid the scoundrels well and gaily skipped to Ahab's room and said, "To Ahab, the King of Israel, I present to you Naboth's vineyard which you wanted so badly. The man is dead. So it's all yours. I hope the vegetables you plan to grow there are really tasty."

Ahab thanked his wife and went out to inspect his newly acquired property. As he was sauntering about, planning where he would plant the various vegetables, he heard a voice behind him, " Say, King Ahab, sir, after murdering this man are you going to take over his property as well?"

The voice sounded somewhat familiar but he didn't expect this man to be out there in the country. He turned and recognized Elijah, the prophet of Yahweh, "Have you caught up with me, my enemy?"

Enough of the tragic story. What do we see in the mirror? The first thing I see is that Ahab speaks for us, that's right, for you and for me: affluent people. He does not need that vineyard. He has all kinds of gardens, property and wealth and yet he says, " I want, I want." And when he couldn't have his own selfish way he got super depressed, his stomach got upset, he went to his bed, turned to the wall and sulked. Ahab echoes one of the prominent attitudes and obsessions of our time: covetousness. Vernard Eller has identified this as "the hallmark of our society." Commandment number ten warns against it. We as a Menno-nite people were eking out an existence long enough that we didn't think we were susceptible to covetousness. Actually many were, but it starts deep in the heart and doesn't always surface until surplus cash brings on the opportunity to follow up on it. Remember Archie Bunker? He said it too, "Look out for Number 1." Take care of number one first and, if necessary, override the right of others.

Secondly, I see Ahab speaking for the powerful people, the "haves" of the world who have clout in all sorts of ways and use it to their own advantage. What chance did "little Naboth" have against the king who happened to live next door? Not one chance in a million! Jezebel had everything at her fingertips to wipe Naboth off the map quickly so that her covetous, greedy husband could be happy again. She used all the machinery, the clout at her disposal, and the little guy next door was disposed of.

You and I have heard of similar things. We've heard of the debate between aboriginals' claims versus the claims and intentions of gas and oil developers in the north. It is so easy for governments and corporations to ride over the rights of the little guys, in many instances the Native people, and win. We think of Rhodesia some years ago or of South Africa and realize the danger of white power, a minority group which has clout and is willing to subdue and to expropriate the "have nots." And such situations exist not only far from home. The same thing is at work in our congregations. People who have power because of their positions or their wealth and who speak up on issues seem to carry more weight in meetings than the ordinary persons. Others may well think, "If we don't go along with this idea and proposal, then that person may not make as substantial a contribution." And decisions are influenced not on their own merit but on the basis of the voice of powerful people.

Thirdly, I see that Ahab speaks not only for the affluent and the high and mighty but, on a more personal level, he speaks for each of us—not always, but when we become so obsessed with our wants that we do some pretty damaging, destructive things in an attempt to have our own way.

Ahab speaks clearly for the student who wants a good grade but has "goofed off" for months; then is willing to buy that term paper, plagiarize, or cheat on an exam in order to get that B or even an A. And when the teacher or professor returns the essay or the exam it seems as empty a victory as when Ahab stood in his garden that day, confronted by Elijah or by his own searing conscience.

Ahab speaks clearly for the couple from Winnipeg who went to Grand Forks, North Dakota. They so badly wanted that fur-trimmed leather coat for her and that fine pair of leather cowboy boots for him—all for such an incredible saving compared to Winnipeg prices—that they bought the items and wore them, right up to the customs office at Emerson. They did not declare their purchases—after all, they had been worn a few hours already. But there in the "customs vineyard" their little scheme blew up in their faces. They drove back to Winnipeg without their fur-trimmed leather coat and without the leather boots.

Ahab speaks for the person who wants that certain promotion. "I've got to have it, even though I'm not exactly in line for it yet." So schemes are hatched and carried out to discredit the competition. You get the promotion but as you take over in your new office you realize there's a queer taste in your mouth. Elijah, or someone else, must be around somewhere, confronting me with my hollow victory.

Ahab speaks for the husband or wife who, after a number of years of marriage and parenting two children, gets the notion, "I want my self-fulfilment or I'll die." And so in the name of this questionable want a marriage is broken, a family torn apart, and all that one has lived with, strived for, is thrown out the window. And when you stand in your garden of self-fulfilment—wherever that is—you realize that the victory is empty. You have given up too much; you have lost while you thought you were gaining. You gave in to the craving and it did you in.

Ahab may speak to the young man or woman who feels the compulsion to marry. "I want to get married; I have to get married or I'll die." Blinded by this obsession they lose all sense of discrimination and fall for the first person who shows any interest. And in a short time they show up in the pastor's office with, "Oh, we're so madly in love, and we want to get married." Nonsense. You may be mad, but you're not in love!

Ancient Ahab speaks for you and for me, doesn't he? He speaks for groups or nations or individuals whose wants are so strong that they have completely lost their heads. They listen to the crazy ideas, the twisted notions, and the immoral suggestions of a Jezebel who is as unscrupulous as any person can imagine. Ahab knew better and he should have rejected her idea. We know better too, but we too fall for the line of society bent on selfishness, greed and having more and more things. Like Ahab, we "build our own cage out of the bars of unrealistic and unhealthy desires" (Vernard Eller).

Jezebel the schemer, the temptress, appeals to his lust for power, appeals to his selfishness and greed, not to his sense of moral right, "You wouldn't let this little guy stand in your way, would you?"

And the end of the matter? Elijah speaks the word of judgement, "Thus says the Lord, I will bring disaster upon you." There is judgment on immoral behaviour. You cannot break God's laws and expect to go "scott free." A time of reckoning will surely come. And that is as true today as it was then. You and I cannot flaunt God's law and go unscathed. The chapter ends with Ahab as dejected, gloomy and depressed as when it began. But this time for a different reason. He tears his clothes. He knew disaster would strike. Whether he was only sorry he was caught, or sorry for what he had done, we do not know.

We have a choice about how we will manage our lives, how we will function as stewards of that which is entrusted to us. Ahab's way is one option, Paul's is another: "I have learned to be satisfied with what I have. I know what it is to be in need and what it is to have more than enough. I have learned the secret, so that anywhere, at any time I am content, whether I am full or hungry, whether I have too much or too little. I have the strength to face all conditions by the power that Christ gave me" (Philippians 4:11–13).

How different Ahab's life would have been if he had been able to say, "I have learned to be satisfied with what I have, to be content." Then desire would not have become deadly obsession, blinding him to the rights of others.

Paul had little reason to speak the way he did. He was in prison guarded by a Roman soldier. Ahab was captivated by the prison of his own desires. Ahab had so much of this world's goods, Paul so very little. He worked as a tent-maker when he needed some cash. On one occasion Paul said, "I have been hungry and thirsty, I have often been without food and shelter or clothing" (2 Corinthians 11:27). Yet Paul could say, "I have learned to be content." Ahab, who had so much reason to be satisfied, was not content.

Contentment and happiness do not rest in the number of things we own or hope to own. The basis for contentment lies elsewhere. Ahab's life ended in disaster and the judgement which was deferred fell on his sons. Paul's life, on the other, had ended in victory, "I have fought the good fight, I have finished the race, I have kept the faith. Henceforth there is laid up for me the crown of righteousness" (2 Timothy 4:7)—words which Ahab could never utter, even though he had a crown. One ancient writer said of Ahab, "There was no one who had devoted himself so completely to doing wrong in the Lord's sight as Ahab" (1 Kings 21:25).

What had Paul learned that gave him contentment amidst uncertainty and hardship, which gave him freedom and joy even in a prisoner's cell? Was it not that Paul had accepted Jesus' teaching that persons are of infinitely more worth than things or property? In other words, he had sorted out his priorities. Much in our society tries to con us into accepting the view that more and better and newer things and property spell meaning and happiness. That was Ahab's line.

Both Paul and Ahab had consuming passions in line with their real priorities. Ahab destroyed people in order to gain things; Paul lived in service to people—living not to accumulate earthly treasures but to proclaim the release from selfishness and sin. Paul's secret was to live strengthened by Christ, directed by him who gave himself without limit to the world.

Ahab's story touches your life and mine. Has the mirror which is Ahab's tragic life alerted us to take stock of where we are going? Paul stands before us with an invitation and an opportunity: to reject Ahab's way, to accept Christ's way, to let him who is the Lord of true freedom free us from the captivities of our own making, free us from the bondage to things to a life of service to others.

5

MUCH IS GIVEN—MUCH IS REQUIRED

Much is required from the person to whom much is given; much more is required from the person to whom much more is given (Luke 12:48).

These words of Jesus come at the conclusion of a parable in which the themes of stewardship and trust have been touched on. The verse divides itself into two parts, two aspects which will form the basis for this sermon: "much is given—much is required."

Four things come to mind under the phrase, "much is given."

We have been given a story. It may be striking to us that the main themes of our faith come to us in story form. From earliest childhood we have heard the stories of faith. Our parents, our teachers and church have transmitted this heritage to us.

In his Pentecost sermon, Peter summarized the story thus:

. . . Jesus of Nazareth, a man attested to you by God with deeds of power, wonder and signs that God did through him among you, as you yourselves know—this man, handed over to you according to the definite plan and foreknowledge of God, you crucified and killed by the hands of those outside the law. . . . This Jesus God raised up, and of that all of us are witness. Being therefore exalted at the right hand of God, and having received from the Father the promise of the Holy Spirit, he has poured out this that you both see and hear (Acts 2:22–23, 32–33).

This is the centre of our faith. An invaluable treasure has been given to us. Through the story we discover who the Lord is, what his stance and attitude toward us are, and that we can turn to him in faith and receive both forgiveness for sin and guidance for life. This is the most important thing for which we ought to be thankful in the story: the treasures of faith.

But our text does not permit us merely to be grateful. Jesus said, "to whom much is given, *much will be required.*" Having received so

---

First preached in October 1981 at First Mennonite Church, Winnipeg, Manitoba.

much carries obligations, responsibilities, requirements as well. Anyone who is offended by the second half of this verse must look into his/her own heart and seriously ask, "Am I truly grateful?" Those who are truly thankful are glad to hear about the requirements which go along with the blessings.

Since we have been recipients of the story of faith, some requirements are laid upon us: to recommit ourselves, to dedicate ourselves to serve the Lord; to continue to immerse ourselves in the story; to continue to express our faith in our lives; to share the story of faith with others. Is that expecting too much? Not if we are truly thankful.

We have received much in terms of material wealth. In spite of the fact that we complain about increasing costs, inflation and rising interest rates, we must admit, "We've never had it so good." We cannot begin to list all of the things we take for granted in our lives. Certainly there are differences among us—some have more and some have a little less—but most of us have more than ever before.

But we crave more and strive for more. Opportunities abound and we continue to acquire. We replace, retire, redecorate, remodel, relocate and try to rejuvenate ourselves as well as our possessions. On the one hand we enjoy the possibilities, yet in our saner moments we also recognize that these endless possibilities are a snare. Materialism and covetousness can take us prisoner all too quickly. The Bible recognizes this problem, alerts us to it and warns us about it. Yes, we are to receive and enjoy this bounty, but in the midst of enjoying it we are not to forget the Lord (Deuteronomy 8:11–19).

In reference to the material bounty we have received, we too have responsibilities. The Bible doesn't simply treat us as lucky and irresponsible recipients. We are also stewards or managers of the entrusted bounty. What might that mean? That our appetites be curbed; that we be generous in our giving, convinced that with our monies we can support the work of the church, our private schools, relief efforts and mission work in many places.

We need to be reminded in this regard that if we are giving the same amount today as five years ago, then we are actually giving considerably less than before. Our giving should at least keep up with increases in inflation—that would be the minimum. Actually, it should increase more than that—our incomes have and so have the opportunities and needs to do good. Is this expecting too much? Not if we are truly thankful for all that we have received.

We have been blessed with relationship—with others, in families, with friends. This aspect of receiving is not as concrete as the material bounty we've just considered, but it is of much greater importance. The relationship between spouses, family members and friends are among the most important things in life. If these connections are satisfying, then we can cope with anything. If they are not, then all of life goes sour. Relationships include trust, openness, self-disclosure, love and communication. In his great chapter on love (1 Corinthians 13), Paul makes the statement, "If I have not love, I am a noisy gong." I would like to change that and say, "If I have no close relationships with others, then my life is barren."

Here too there is poverty and abundance. Some find relating easy. Others are clumsy at it. We all know how badly it feels when a relationship is uncertain, especially with someone that matters a lot to us. Relationships have been given to us; let us be thankful for them.

It would be good to take a sheet of paper and list persons who are meaningful in our lives, then go through the list, pausing at each name and asking, "Am I thankful for what this person means to me? Is our relationship in order? Can we fellowship on a deep level or are there issues that are untouchable? What can I do to promote this relationship, to deepen it?" So often we feel positively about someone but keep our feelings a secret. If we are thankful, let us show it by saying it directly to the person involved.

But here too it is not enough to be thankful. More than that is required. We are challenged to love others as ourselves; we are challenged to let a relationship cost us something—in time and energy; we are challenged to seek the other person's interest first. Then we will always seek peace and pursue it with vigour. Is this expecting too much? Not if we are truly thankful for relationships given to us.

There is still more. Not only the story of faith, not only material bounty, not only relationship with others—*hardships and difficulties also have been given to us.* Here we think of other immaterial things, yet which are very important: things that cause us anxiety, stress and despair.

The New Testament urges us to thank God in all things, in all circumstances. Some of life's most valuable lessons are learned nowhere else but in the crucible of suffering. Usually when some difficulty comes our way, we ask, "Why? Why did God let this happen?" It may be more productive to ask, "What might the Lord be able to show me through this experience?"

It may be a grief, an injury, an illness, a setback, failure to succeed—these too are among "the givens" of life. How we respond to them makes all the difference in the world. In such experiences we humbly accept God's grace and the support of friends. We dip deeply into the resources of both our faith and our relationships.

Here too there are expectations of us. We become recipients of difficulty, but we are expected to be stewards as well, stewards who have discovered something about God's presence and the mystery of life which we would not learn on Easy Street. Paul gives the experience of suffering a strange twist: "who comforts us in all our affliction"—so that we will feel better? No—"so that we may be able to comfort those who are in any affliction, with the comfort with which we ourselves are comforted by God" (2 Corinthians 1:4). What we gain through the experience of suffering is to be of benefit to others who experience difficulty.

This actually happens. How often when we go to see someone who has had real difficulty we discover that we have been helped, encouraged, strengthened in faith by the one we had gone to cheer up. So, if you have learned something through a difficult experience, don't keep it all to yourself. Share it. Is this expecting too much? Not if we are truly thankful in difficult circumstances.

The words of our text are few, but they probe deeply. They remind us of many things we have received and of which we are stewards: story, bounty, relationships and difficulties. And they challenge us to acknowledge the requirements that belong to gratitude. May the Spirit of God embed these words in our hearts that they may bear fruit in our lives.

6

CELEBRATE THE BOUNTY

*Make a joyful noise to the Lord, all the earth. Worship the Lord
with gladness; come into his presence with singing. Know that
the Lord is God. It is he that made us, and we are his; we are his
people, and the sheep of his pasture. Enter his gates with
thanksgiving, and his courts with praise. Give thanks to him,
bless his name For the Lord is good; his steadfast love endures
forever, and his faithfulness to all generations* (Psalm 100).

*When you have come into the land that the Lord your God is
giving you as an inheritance to possess, and you possess it, and
settle in it, you shall take some of the first of all the fruit of the
ground, which you harvest from the land that the Lord your God
is giving you, and you shall put it in a basket and go to the place
that the Lord your God will choose as a dwelling for his name.
You shall go to the priest who is in office at that time, and say to
him, "Today I declare to the Lord your God that I have come into
the land that the Lord swore to our ancestors to give us." When
the priest takes the basket from your hand and sets it down before
the altar of the Lord your God, you shall make this response
before the Lord your God: "A wandering Aramean was my
ancestor; he went down into Egypt and lived there as an alien,
few in number, and there he became a great nation, mighty and
populous. When the Egyptians treated us harshly and afflicted us,
by imposing hard labour on us, we cried to the Lord, the God of
our ancestors; the Lord heard our voice and saw our affliction,
our toil, and our oppression. The Lord brought us out of Egypt
with a mighty hand and an outstretched arm, with a terrifying
display of power, and with signs and wonders; and he brought us
into this place and gave us this land, a land flowing with milk
and honey. So now I bring the first of the fruit of the ground that
you, O Lord, have given me." You shall set it down before the
Lord your God and bow down before the Lord your God. Then*

First preached in October 1995 at Bethel Mennonite Church, Winnipeg,
Manitoba.

you together with the Levites and the aliens who reside among you, shall celebrate with all the bounty that the Lord your God has given to you and to your house (Deuteronomy 26:1–11).

Rejoice in the Lord always; again I will say, Rejoice. Let your gentleness be known to everyone. The Lord is near. Do not worry about anything, but in everything by prayer and supplication with thanksgiving let your requests be made known to God. And the peace of God, which surpasses all understanding, will guard your hearts and your minds in Christ Jesus. Finally, beloved, whatever is true, whatever is honourable, whatever is just, whatever is pure, whatever is pleasing, whatever is commendable, if there is any excellence and if there is anything worthy of praise, think about these things. Keep on doing the things that you have learned and received and heard and seen in me, and the God of peace will be with you (Philippians 4:4–9).

Celebrating Thanksgiving is complicated even though it appears simple; it is difficult even though it seems to be straightforward. Why? Because we are invited to remember the past. And when we do this, we recall the good and pleasant things as well as the not so good and the painful things that are part of each of our lives. This remembering is front and centre in the text from Deuteronomy.

In his book, *In the Name of Jesus,* Henri Nouwen writes: ". . . beneath the pleasantries of daily life there are many gaping wounds that carry such names as: abandonment, betrayal, rejection, rupture and loss. These . . . reveal the darkness that never completely leaves the human heart" (Nouwen: 26). This is profound insight that, while we celebrate the bounty, we do not, we cannot, forget the pain, our own woundedness which never seems to leave us.

The call to worship, the hymns and the choir anthems in our worship services urge us to be thankful, but for some this may be difficult. We may be irritated by the texts—all calling us to be thankful. For some the whole notion of celebrating the bounty which the Lord has given is a source of irritation—nothing more.

If you are one who has come to this service with disappointment in your heart, or with the feeling of desolation, or with the profound sense of depression, feeling down about things, about others, about life, about the future, or if you have come with a full dose of desperation, you don't know what you're going to do next, where you will turn to deal with the issues in your life, then you might be irritated with this whole idea of celebrating the bounty. If you have come today with feelings of frustration, failure, fear or fury about someone or something in your life, you might well be irritated with this call to rehearse life and to celebrate the bounty. And yet, that is *exactly* the point of our text.

Thanksgiving might be complicated from another angle as well: if things are going well with you. If you have your work, your spouse, your family and friends, your hobbies, you might not feel irritated but you might feel a little guilty. Guilty, that things are going so well when you know full well how others are struggling and you are not; how others are ill, and you enjoy health; how others live under an ominous dark cloud and you are walking in the sunshine—then you and I might feel guilty.

Whether we are among those who feel irritated or those who feel a bit of guilt, all of us must come to grips with the message of this text in which we read the words, "celebrate all the bounty." What does this *not* mean?

Celebrating the bounty does *not* mean that we as Christians are to do what many in our culture do: live for profits so we have more bounty to celebrate; or acquire more and more possessions and prove that "covetousness has become the hallmark of our society" (Vernard Eller). While our text speaks about the blessing of living in a land "flowing with milk and honey," it does not mean that we adopt our culture's compulsive striving, as one writer has put it: "the relentless quest for goods, property, and possessions." That would not be what we have in mind by celebrating the bounty.

Nor does celebrating the bounty mean gathering those of like means around us, having a cosy group of like-minded and similarly affluent friends in or out for a sumptuous meal, celebrating the wealth that has been given—but in a very self-centred and limited way.

Nor does celebrating the bounty mean getting to the top of whatever ladder we're on in our profession, among our peers, in business, or rejoicing that finally we have acquired that piece of real estate we've worked for so long and which is suitable to our current status in life, since this signals that we are keeping up with those we want to be seen keeping up with.

Nor is celebrating the bounty talking to ourselves the way the rich farmer in Jesus' parable talked to himself, "Soul, you have ample goods laid up for many years; relax, eat, drink and be merry" (Luke 12:19). Like the farmer, it's in reference to our possessions that we do the most talking. We carry on a very important and highly revealing soliloquy with ourselves about our good fortune and about what we expect to acquire in the future. This man in the parable received an F from the

Lord, "Failure, you fool." He thought he was truly celebrating the bounty but he was not. He had forgotten some of the important things in our text which has different notions about "celebrating the bounty."

First, celebrating the bounty involves remembering and rehearsing the story-line of life already past, not only one's own but also the life of one's forebears, the ones who had wilderness experiences. Note the following:

> A wandering Aramean was my ancestor; he went down into Egypt and lived there as an alien, few in number, and there he became a great nation, mighty and populous. When the Egyptians treated us harshly and afflicted us by imposing hard labour on us, we cried to the Lord, the God of our ancestors; the Lord heard our voice and saw our affliction, our toil and our oppression. The Lord brought us out of Egypt . . . and gave us this land, a land flowing with milk and honey. So now I bring the first of the fruit of the land that you, O Lord, have given me (Deuteronomy 26: 5–10).

Compare this with the man in Jesus' parable: "Soul, you have ample goods laid up for many years, relax, eat, drink, be merry." In this insightful soliloquy, the man is talking to himself while the man in our text is addressing his words to God in the presence of another, the priest, in the ritual of worship. The man in Jesus' story lived within a very limited horizon—he drew a tight circle around himself—while the man in Deuteronomy had a wide horizon and included in his life's story-line his ancestors as well as his contemporary community.

If we really want to "celebrate the bounty" of our lives, the first thing we will need to do is to slow down enough to remember, to rehearse the story that is life. "I remember . . ." and our minds go back and we name the harshness of life only decades ago, the affliction that was ours in each family circle. We will remember how our fathers and mothers, like the Israelites, cried to the Lord their God—and their cries were heard. Since then we have prospered, we have been blessed. Today, with these things brought into conscious memory, we celebrate that bountiful blessing by doing what that person did: bring the first of the fruit of the land.

Second, in remembering the past—our own and our peoples'—we find release from resentments, memories and grudges—those things which keep us in prison all the days of our lives. The Israelite coming to worship could come year after year with a deep-seated grudge against the Egyptian experience when the Israelites had been treated like dirt by their overlords. Or they could find release from those memories, not obliterating them, but having the sting of them removed. I am not suggesting that we cover up or excuse or whitewash the past, but that we really deal with it and arrive at the point of forgiveness, of letting it go, of bringing something to closure, and going on with the rest of life, knowing that this thing, whatever it is in our lives, has been dealt with.

Thirdly, celebrating the bounty means more than remembering and rehearsing the story-line of life; it means more than dealing with the pain of the past; it means gladly admitting, no longer denying, but admitting before others that we, you and I, have been richly blessed and that we are thankful for the material blessings, for spiritual blessings and guidance, for salvation through Christ, for peace in our hearts and hope for time and eternity. To celebrate the bounty, and not feel guilty about it, we recognize publicly that God "richly provides us with everything," as Paul put it, "for our enjoyment" (1 Timothy 6:17).

Recall Ebenezer Scrooge in Charles Dickens' *Christmas Carol*. Once he was converted he was so overwhelmed by joy, he could not contain himself. He celebrated his bounty, not by pretending he didn't have much, but by giving generously to his family and his employees, opening the treasures of his heart and his hands.

Fourthly, celebrating the bounty is more than remembering and rehearsing, more than letting go of painful memories, more than admitting that we have been richly blessed; it is responding generously with a sacrifice of thanksgiving. This is not speaking those foolish words the farmer spoke to himself: "Soul, you have ample goods laid up for many years." Rather, "I bring the first fruit of the land which you, O Lord, have given me." To really celebrate the bounty we must have the underlying conviction, the biblical notion, that all that we have is given; all has been received from the hand of God. Certainly, we worked, we studied, we toiled, we kept at it, yet beneath and beyond all of our own efforts, we as Christians have this surprising attitude, "All that I have is a gift; I am the grateful recipient; I am not the master, not the owner."

On the one hand that is easy to say, but it does not remain easy. After we have admitted the bounty of material and spiritual blessing, we are reminded of Jesus' word when he said, "Freely you have received, freely give." To hoard the bounty we have been given in life, like the foolish farmer, is to live life as a failure and receive an F.

In the public act of bringing his basket to the priest, the ancient Israelite symbolized something very important: the breaking of the power of possessions over his spirit. Jacques Ellul has said that our wealth has to be dressed up, to be "clothed with grace." And that is done by breaking the grip of our possessions on us, not by hoarding for ourselves but joyfully insisting that a portion will be given—and thus the spell of materialism and self-centredness is broken. By giving the portion, the worshipper symbolized that he was consecrating the whole, his life, in service to the Lord and others.

Donald Hinze writes: "Christianity is a burden, as long as we are ungenerous, pinched and cramped in our giving." We know that giving is the path toward true joy and meaning in life, yet as believers we have done relatively little to show by our generosity that the power of the material over us has been broken. Our local church budgets, our conferences, our schools are all in need of sustained financial support, and we are more affluent than ever, have more double-income families than before, but if statistics are reliable we are told that we do not give anywhere near 10 percent on average. There are exceptions to be sure, but many, too many, give below 3 percent. I pray that we could experience a revival one of these years—a revival related to the conversion of the pocket book—and that we would be able to see in every church and on every conference level and in every institution what Jesus meant when he said, "Give and it will be given to you, good measure, pressed down, shaken together, running over. . . . For the measure you give will be the measure you get back" (Luke 6:38). Or, as Malachi the prophet put it, "Put me to the test, says the Lord of hosts, if I will not open the windows of heaven for you and pour down for you an overflowing blessing" (Malachi 3:10).

Fifthly, celebrating the bounty means more than remembering, releasing, admitting, sacrificing—it means a whole lot more. Notice what the last verse in Deuteronomy says: "Then you, together with the Levites and the aliens who reside among you, shall celebrate" (v.11). The ancient Israelite is commanded to celebrate the bounty—not by excluding the less fortunate, those Levites and aliens who were dependent on the rest, those aliens who had no voice in the assembly—no, they were to be included in the celebration of the bounty. This suggests that, while we are to be deeply grateful for all we have been blessed with, we are never to fall into the trap of forgetting the less fortunate, those who feel voiceless, who live on the edges as aliens always do, the needy near by and the needy far away. What a powerful text! What a testimony to all of us, these 11 verses telling us so much about our obligation to be stewards because we worship the Lord who is utterly faithful to us.

Let's sum it up this way: All of us can walk with the Israelite to the place of worship, remembering, releasing, admitting, thanking and facing the incredible challenge later uttered by Paul: "God richly provides us with everything for our enjoyment," and with that blessing we "are to do good, to be rich in good works, generous, and ready to share" (1 Timothy 6:17–18). That is the way to celebrate the bounty. May each of us learn to live this way to the glory of God and for the good of others.

7

TOWARD A THEOLOGY OF FUNDRAISING

In November 1991 on the occasion of the MEDA Convention in Lancaster, Pennsylvania, a small group consisting of Gary Franz (General Conference), Ron Loeppky (Conference of Mennonites in Canada), Marlin Miller (Associated Mennonite Biblical Seminary) and John Neufeld (Canadian Mennonite Bible College), met to discuss individual fundraising, overlap, duplication of efforts and competition between fundraising efforts and fund raisers. At that meeting Marlin and John were given the task of drafting a statement on the theology of fundraising. This draft was shared with the others at the Sioux Falls (South Dakota) Conference during the week of July 20–26, 1992. There it was decided to consider it again during the MEDA Convention in Denver, Colorado, October 29–November 1, 1992.

History and background. Generally, our Anabaptist-Mennonite forebears owned property and considered themselves stewards who were called by God to serve God and others with their resources. According to the article, "Stewardship" in *Mennonite Encyclopedia* V, Swiss applicants for baptism were asked "whether they would conse-crate themselves with all their temporal possessions to the service of God and his people" (859). Dutch Mennonites even provided aid for their enemies (the Reformed) who found themselves in an emergency situation. Later, some of those whom the Mennonites helped betrayed them to the authorities. The Hutterites developed an alternative to holding property in private and practised community of goods. Although these examples do not relate directly to fundraising in the contemporary North American sense, they do demonstrate an attitude toward material possessions which differs significantly from that of many North American Mennonites.

In the Russian Mennonite experience, worship services did not include the offering as we have come to know it in the North American setting. Members were assessed church dues on an annual basis to cover

An essay written by Marlin Miller and John Neufeld; final version presented on October 29–November, 1992, at the MEDA Convention, Denver, Colorado.

the cost of operating the local church and meeting the needs of the poor. In addition to the dues expected from everyone for covering of basic expenses, members were also invited to contribute to special projects according to interest and ability. A box for offerings and dues was located at the exit of the church for the convenience of the members. Larger projects like the building of churches, schools, hospitals and other facilities were funded by appeals to the wealthier members of the congregation. It seems that this was done by approaching those members on an individual basis. This is confirmed in a recent article by James Urry: "Although the contributions of individual Mennonites and small groups provided continuous support, the large donations made by wealthy individuals proved essential for the establishment of and major capital expenditures of most institutions" (*The Cost of Community: The Funding and Economic Management of the Russian Commonwealth before 1914*, 42).

This basic approach to funding remained common among Canadian Mennonites who had Russian roots. Shortly after mid-century, steward-ship education, preaching and teaching entered our churches. The itinerant ministry of Milo Kauffman at the Vancouver Mennonite Mission Church in 1957 is one example of this new development. His intention and practice were clear—to clearly teach and preach the principles of Christian stewardship and to motivate his hearers to commit themselves to live as responsible stewards. This had a significant impact on all who heard him.

It was during those years that the unified budget came to be dominant in the Conference of Mennonites in Canada. Among the MCs the move to unified budgets came especially between 1961 and 1971 when all three of the district conferences moved in that direction as the result of a lay stewardship council made up of representatives of the district conferences and appointed by the General Board. It was also in this period that Lester Janzen was appointed Stewardship Secretary by the General Conference Mennonite Church. For several decades Conference programs and institutions relied almost exclusively on appeals to the member congregations for funds to do the work of the Conference through the unified budget. However, there have always been exceptions: Commission on Overseas Mission (COM), Mennonite Biblical Seminary (MBS) and Canadian Mennonite Bible College (CMBC) solicited funds more directly: by mail, in personal contacts, by appeals for above-budget giving for specific projects in public meetings, or through other public means such as church periodicals or bulletin inserts. It must also be added that special capital projects were funded by special fund drives. In some instances an additional amount for a building project was actually added to the amount that the conference budget expected from each congregation.

While the various levels of conference relied primarily on the unified budget for support, a variety of interdenominational and parachurch agencies and religious broadcasters (radio and TV) engaged in direct solicitation among our members with considerable success. This activity and its results did not go unnoticed by those in leadership positions.

In the 1980s our Conferences faced a somewhat new economic and fiscal situation. It was a time of inflation, high interest rates and economic uncertainty. The annual budget increases no longer kept pace with the increases in operating expenditures. As an example was the situation facing CMBC in 1986. There was an ever widening gap between annual expenses and income. The College faced several options at this time: to request a larger percentage of CMC donations; to increase its fees drastically; to reduce its academic program and begin releasing faculty; to lobby the provincial government for an annual grant; or to seek additional funding from its corporate and individual supporters.

The Conference was unwilling to enlarge the CMBC portion of its budget; and the College feared that an increase in fees would negatively impact enrolment. It was also considered suicidal to reduce its program and its faculty. The decision was made to continue to lobby the government for an annual grant (together with other church-related colleges), and to approach supporters in the private and business sector for additional contributions. This decision was not made lightly since it did signal a shift away from the unified budget, which had served the Conference so well, in the direction of one-on-one fundraising. A GC publication on fundraising mentions this shift: "In Mennonite churches in Canada this trend (toward individual fundraising) has been less prevalent but is beginning to grow. Church-wide and area conferences now wrestle with the tension of trying to attract gifts from individuals while remaining predominantly dependent on congregational giving and goodwill" ("A Philosophy of Fund Raising for the General Conference Mennonite Church," 1992).

During the 1970s and 1980s Mennonites in Canada experienced a rapid rise in their financial resources. In part this was due to making the appropriate decisions, but mostly it was the result of being in a situation where property values appreciated sharply and incomes rose along with the high inflation and interest rates. Some realized that they were now in a situation of having considerably more discretion regarding their spending. They simply had more than they needed for routine personal and family expenses. More Mennonites than ever before in the Canadian experience had become affluent.

According to Kauffman and Driedger's study, *The Mennonite Mosaic,* North American Mennonites are now more affluent than ever. Between 1971 and 1988 the median household income increased 17 percent in real income. In 1971 the median income amounted to $9,608; in 1988, to $31,123 (figures in US dollars). The average income for Mennonites in Canada in 1989 was $34,845 (Cdn $ @.85 exchange = $29,618 US). Simultaneously the percentage of households that estimated their level of charitable giving as 5 percent or more has declined in the past 20 years. In 1972, 63 percent of GCMC households gave 5 percent or more; in 1989, only 55 percent gave at those levels. In 1972, 66 percent of MC households gave 5 percent or more; in 1989, 65 percent.

In spite of these statistics, the increase in affluence led to a new situation in the local churches. While many of the members were strong supporters of their local church budgets, they realized that if they contributed as much as they were able to the local budget it would be badly skewed. They continued to give their fair share to the local budget, then gave additional monies to special projects on the basis of interest and need.

Rationale for giving. It is interesting to note that, although significant attention has recently been given to a theology of stewardship, there has not been a parallel effort regarding a theology of fundraising. In the document entitled, "A Philosophy of Fund Raising for the General Conference Mennonite Church," we read, "Although significant attention in recent years has been on how to increase solicitation of gifts from individuals, the congregational support base continues and will continue to be crucial." In reference to a rationale for this shift, the document does not develop a theology, but identifies some ideas: "Following are some ideas that have guided efforts in this area: that trust should be developed between the fund raiser and the potential donor; that giving should be without pressure; that the donor should have ties to a GC church; and that the future financial well-being of the donor be preserved." It is surprising that the request for the writing of a theology of fundraising has not been expressed earlier in our development.

Biblical basis for a theology of fundraising. It seems that the theology of fundraising should be closely related to a theology of stewardship. The whole notion of stewardship should be tied to our understanding of the mission of the church in the world. Money is one of the resources which enables the church to carry out its mission of inviting others to faith and serving in the name of Christ. The scope of stewardship teaching will need to include dealing with issues related to fundraising.

There is considerable material in the Bible giving both explicit and implicit teaching on the theme of stewardship, but it is much more difficult to find passages which deal with the theme of fundraising. Exodus 34–35 tells of resource raising for the building of the tabernacle. In the New Testament there seems to be one major fundraising effort which receives considerable attention in Pauline correspondence. We are referring to the "collection for the saints" and would like to review the material and draw some tentative conclusions and extrapolations from it. The passages in question are Galatians 2:9–10, Romans 15:25–29, 1 Corinthians 16:1–4 and 2 Corinthians 8–9.

Two things must be remembered about Paul in regard to fundraising: 1) he was reluctant to ask for money for his own support, although the record shows that the Philippians did in fact support him (Philippians 4:10–20) and he expressed gratitude for it; and 2) he vigorously and tirelessly worked for the collection of funds for the poor in Jerusalem. Before drawing some conclusions and suggesting some learnings for today, we would like to summarize the situation and its development.

The impetus for this major fundraising effort emerges at the conclusion of the Jerusalem Council. The main issue at the Council was the question whether the Gentile mission had validity or not. The accord that was reached recognized the place of both the Jewish mission under the leadership of Peter and the Gentile mission under Paul's leadership. It was symbolized by "the right hand of fellowship," indicating that Paul should go to the Gentiles and Peter to the circumcised (Galatians 2:9). It was in connection with this accord that Paul recalls the request to collect for the poor, "They asked only one thing, that we remember the poor, which was actually what I was eager to do" (Galatians 2:10).

Some years later, in his letter to the Romans, Paul mentions this fundraising effort and also theologized about its meaning. He uses debtor language and expressions of reciprocity in speaking about the project. The Gentile believers were indebted to the Jewish community for having heard the good news from and through them. They had historical priority and hence the Gentiles were indebted to them. Gratitude for spiritual blessings was to find expression in the giving of their material resources to those who were now in need. This indebtedness was the Gentile side of the reciprocity equation. When the Jewish believers received and accepted the contributions from their Gentile brothers and sisters they, from their side, acknowledged the validity of the Gentile mission. For Paul then, the giving and receiving had become more than giving and receiving; it had become a symbol of the accord reached at the Jerusalem Council.

It is clear that Paul had some anxiety about this theological dimension of the project. In Romans 15:31 he asks that they pray for him, "that my ministry may be acceptable to the saints." Some interpreters understand this to be a clear reference to the uncertainty in his mind: Would the gift of the Gentile churches be acceptable to the Jewish church?

The reference to an embarrassing incident in Antioch, reported in Galatians 2, adds further weight to this concern. The accord about the two-pronged mission of the church was practically feasible when the two groups, Gentiles and Jews, were geographically separate, but on the occasion of a mixed gathering it would surely be tested. Trouble arose when Jews and Gentiles ate together. At first Peter, who was visiting in Antioch, ate (fellowshipped) with the Gentiles, but when some Jewish brothers arrived on the scene he reversed his position and withdrew from the table. For Paul, this was a rupture of the accord reached in Jerusalem, and Paul took Peter to task publicly for his inconsistent behaviour. The collection for the saints, Paul's fundraising project, had now increased in meaning. The collection could become a way of repairing the breach between Gentile and Jewish dimensions of the church's mission.

Let us give our attention now to the Corinthian correspondence regarding the fundraising effort. In 1 Corinthians 16:1–4 Paul offers specific instructions for the completion of the campaign. While he was absent from Corinth, rival apostles came on the scene and disrupted the relationship between Paul and the believers. They seem to have derided him for not accepting remuneration from the church, and raised suspicion whether Paul might have diverted some of the funds he collected for his own use. This is a reasonable deduction from Paul's words in the "painful letter" (2 Corinthians 10–13, especially 2 Corinthians 12:16–18 and 2 Corinthians 8:20–21): "We intend that no one should blame us about this generous gift that we are administering, for we intend to do what is right not only in the Lord's sight but also in the sight of others" (8:20-21). And in his appeal for money he mentions that "their love for him" was being tested by their response.

The conclusion we draw from the evidence is that by the time he writes his longest passage on the subject of giving, the project has acquired several layers of theological meaning. In the book, *God and Mammon,* Joutte M. Bassler describes the language Paul uses as having a "rich theological texture" (Bassler: 42). His appeal for aid to the poor saints in Jerusalem is closely intertwined with a cluster of theological terms and concerns (terms such as: grace, diakonia, euologia [blessing, praise] and leitourgia [service]).

Several other things stand out in these chapters:

1) Paul seeks to awaken interest for the fundraising drive in Corinth by referring to the example of other believers (the Macedonians). They are exemplary on several counts: they gave themselves first to the Lord and then to this ministry; he sees in their response the working of God's grace (overcoming obstacles—their extreme poverty and making visible those Christian virtues which by nature were invisible [faith, speech, knowledge, eagerness]).

2) He raises the issues to a high theological plane by referring next to the example of the Lord, who "though rich became poor for your sakes."

3) There should be a fair balance between "your present abundance and their need" (8:14) (cf., "extreme poverty" in 8:2). Bassler states, "equality begets equality." They are on an equal level spiritually and should be on the material level as well.

4) He gives detailed directions for the gathering of the contributions. This may be a hedge against the potential charge of questionable behaviour in using the funds.

5) He challenges them to give generously and with enthusiasm (2 Corinthians 9:6–7).

6) He affirms that God blesses abundantly, "so that by always having enough of everything you may share abundantly in every good work" (9:8). In other words, God promotes and enables generosity.

7) Giving to others glorifies God (9:13). "An act of charity is thereby transformed into an act of worship" (Bassler: 108).

Guidelines for fundraising today: a sketch

1) One striking impression left by the materials surveyed is that the task of fundraising is compatible with the calling of Christian ministry. Paul, the apostle, missionary, evangelist and writer, did not consider fundraising beneath the dignity of his calling by God and the church.

2) It is helpful to intertwine theological meanings and motivations and terms and the particular needs of a given fundraising project.

3) In Paul's thinking fundraising for a project is translocal within the framework of the larger church. The local congregation is to be aware

of the needs and activities of other parts of the church and see itself as a partner in mission together with other parts of the body of Christ in the world.

4) Fundraising is based on a variety of appeals: a response of God's blessing in one's life, renewed commitment to the Lord, an expression of worship of God, and the helpful examples of other believers. Giving is to be voluntary, proportionate to one's means, and is a response to the actual needs of others. It is helpful to give detailed instructions and clarify one's procedures so as to avoid confusion, suspicion and misunderstanding.

5) Congregations and conferences should encourage goals for proportionate giving to congregational and broader church projects and ministry. Theologically, the church is much larger than the local congregation. Although it is difficult to make hard and fast rules for relative distribution between local and translocal support, we propose the following guidelines as a way of living out the broader church reality as far as stewardship is concerned: for every two dollars given for local mission and ministry, the goal for *small congregations* should be one dollar for broader church mission (this could also be the place to begin for larger congregations who aren't yet so oriented); for every dollar given for local mission and ministry, the goal for *medium-sized congregations* should be a dollar for broader church mission and ministry; *larger congregations* should aim to give at least 60 percent of every dollar to broader church mission and ministry. Helping congregations and conferences move in these directions should be the task of pastors and others. Conference and institutional fundraisers could help to develop this kind of broader vision and help potential donors see their contributions within the broader picture.

6) Church agencies and institutions should provide honest reporting and projections in church papers and in communication with congregations. The reporting and projections should include percentages of budgets that depend upon church and individual contributions as well as annual results. Giving is one of the few ways people can "vote" on broader church programs. One can see this kind of "voting" as putting the various agencies and institutions in competition with each other—and to some degree it is. One can also see it as presenting the case, reporting and letting people vote with their actions of providing or withholding support. Perhaps the General Conference Mennonite Church (GCMC) should report on all the dollars that are given to GCMC and GC-related agencies and institutions by GCMC congregations and persons (both the amounts and the projects supported).

Another way of communicating and getting feed-back is precisely through the personal contacts by fund-raisers. Their ministry is not only to raise money, but also to report on the stewardship of resources.

7) It may also be appropriate to suggest some guidelines for individual giving to local and broader church mission and ministries. For example, persons whose annual income is average (see figures above) should be encouraged to tithe and give primarily through the local congregational giving (budget or otherwise). Persons who have annual incomes of, say $50,000 or $60,000 or more, should be encouraged to give proportionately out of their income over and above that figure directly to broader church mission and ministry. This would avoid some of the problems (skewing mentioned earlier) in local congregational settings with persons who have more resources. Also, it would communicate to all that "to those whom much has been given, more is expected."

8) Church agencies and church or church-related institutions should have policy statements which indicate the degree to which individual donors may influence program by making significant contributions. Generally speaking, these policies should maximize board/commission control of priorities and minimize control of large donors. Such policy statements are particularly important for naming or not naming buildings or designated endowment funds after donors.

Education
and
Church Leadership

8

THE STORY THAT SHAPES US

Hear, O Israel: The Lord is our God, the Lord alone. You shall love the Lord your God with all your heart, and with all your soul, and with all your might. Keep these words that I am commanding you today in your heart. Recite them to your children and talk about them when you are at home and when you are away, when you lie down and when you rise. Bind them as a sign on your hand, fix them as an emblem on your forehead, and write them on the doorposts of your house and on your gates. . . . When your children ask you in time to come, "What is the meaning of the decrees and the statutes and the ordinances that the Lord our God has commanded you?" then you shall say to your children, "We were Pharaoh's slaves in Egypt, but the Lord brought us out of Egypt with a mighty hand. The Lord displayed before our eyes great and awesome signs and wonders against Egypt, against Pharaoh and all his household. He brought us out from there in order to bring us in, to give us the land that he promised on oath to our ancestors. Then the Lord commanded us to observe all these statutes, to fear the Lord our God, for our lasting good, so as to keep us alive, as is now the case. If we diligently observe this entire commandment before the Lord our God, as he has commanded us, we will be in the right" (Deuteronomy 6:4–9, 20–25).

. . . things that we have heard and known, that our ancestors have told us. We will not hide them from their children; we will tell to the coming generation the glorious deeds of the Lord, and his might, and the wonders that he has done. He established a decree in Jacob, and appointed a law in Israel, which he commanded our ancestors to teach to their children; that the next generation might know them, the children yet unborn, and rise up and tell them to their children, so that they should set their hope

---

Preached in September 1995 at the opening program of Swift Current (Saskatchewan) Bible Institute; adapted from a sermon first preached in January 1982 at First Mennonite Church, Winnipeg, Manitoba.

in God, and not forget the works of God, and keep his command-
ments; and that they should not be like their ancestors, a
stubborn and rebellious generation, a generation whose heart
was not steadfast, whose spirit was not faithful to God (Psalm
78:3–8).
    As you therefore have received Christ Jesus the Lord, continue
to live your lives in him, rooted and built up in him and estab-
lished in the faith, just as you were taught, abounding in thanks-
giving (Colossians 2:6–7).

Centuries ago in Old Testament times a group of 12 men was sent to
check out the land of Palestine on behalf of Israel. When they returned
they came with two reports, one by the majority, the other by the
minority. Part of the majority report went like this: "The land . . .
devours its inhabitants; and all the people we saw were of great stature,
. . . and we seemed ourselves like grasshoppers, and so we seemed to
them" (Numbers 13:32–33). Let's call this the grasshopper syndrome:
the reaction of some in the faith community who become aware of
giants in the land, aware of the odds stacked against them, and they feel
like grasshoppers, quite unable and totally unprepared to address the
challenge before them.
    In many instances this is an accurate description of the mood, the
state, the attitude of Christians and churches in our time. We feel
overwhelmed. We think back and lament the loss of our closed
communities, the loss of isolated living, the loss of being separate from
the world, of knowing where the boundaries and limits are.
    For decades now, at least since the 1950s, we have been moving
more and more into the mainstream of our society and culture. We used
to know pretty well how to share our faith with the next generation. But
now, we seem to be at a loss. We hear statistics and read comments
which become depressing; they drain us of our energies. We are
inclined to throw up our hands in despair and succumb to the grasshopper syndrome, as ancient Israel did.
    Some of the giants we face, within and outside the church are these:
secularism: living as though God were not in the picture; pluralism: a
realization that there are many ways to make sense out of life; relativism: truth depends on where you are, on your culture or situations;
individualism: right and wrong are determined by personal opinion
(Donald Posterski in *True to You* writes,"Relativism accelerates
individualism, fuels uncertainty, and fragments life" [58]); affluence:
radically different than 30 years ago; and increasing biblical illiteracy.

As we notice all these changes it's no wonder we succumb to the grasshopper syndrome. But is that the only option we have? Is the grasshopper feeling the only response to the forces that threaten our very existence? Many of the people complained against Moses and Aaron for bringing them away from Egypt, but some would not give in to the evidence around them. One of their leaders, Joshua, was given the encouragement to move forward and later, as they stood on the verge of moving in, was told: "Be strong and of good courage, be not frightened, neither be dismayed; for the Lord your God is with you wherever you go" (Joshua 1:9).

As people of faith we face a choice: do we give in to the grasshopper syndrome of the many or do we move forward with God's help? I would like to challenge all of us to recommit ourselves to casting off the grasshopper attitude and joining hands and hearts together to face the challenge.

Deep down every person wants something solid to hold on to. We do not want to be endlessly "chasing after wind" (Ecclesiastes 2:14).We want some stars to steer by across the trackless wastes; we want a road map which will direct us across the wilderness that our lives and our time have become. Posterski writes that years ago "captains needed navigational charts to steer their way through rocky channels, . . . trappers in the north required compasses to plot their paths on overcast days. . . . And certainly in the future we will need charts and compasses to navigate our way through the increasing disarray and diversity that confronts and sometimes confuses us" (Posterski, *True to You*: 34).

We give up "chasing after wind," we find the charts and the maps and the compasses we need for meaningful living by turning to the narrative found in scripture and by allowing the biblical story to shape us for life in our time. We commit ourselves to follow the one who is at the centre of that story, Jesus himself.

Again and again we are shaped by that to which we give attention. We know this to be true: some peoples' minds and emotions are being shaped predominantly by soap operas on TV, or by sports, or by one talk show after another. None of these can be our primary shaping influence if we are committed to Christ and the church. We are shaped for life by that which we choose to give attention to, consciously and repeatedly, in community with others, not only as solitary individuals. This is what the texts above are telling us. The goal posed in Colossians 2:6–7 is one of "being rooted and built up in him, and established in the faith." Is this not what we hope and aim for in our Christian life?

The commitment expressed in Psalm 78—which is an incredible

Psalm of religious education—is that the adults in the community of faith will not renege on their God-given responsibility to tell the next generation what they have heard and believed: "We will tell to the coming generation the glorious deeds of the Lord . . . so that they should set their hope in God, and not forget the works of God" (v. 4,7). And did you notice the condition that has to be met before this goal can be reached? They will recall, remember, review what they have heard from their forebears; that is, the story of faith, with the obligation to share it with the upcoming generation.

The text in Deuteronomy 6 tells us something of the preconditions that need to be attended to as well as the dialogical process that is used in telling the next generation about the works of God. Notice that the basis for all Christian education is that adults love the Lord their God with heart and soul and might; they keep the commandments in their hearts—at the centre of their being and life. They are conversant with their faith: recite and talk about it and use symbols to express their heart's commitment in the family setting.

In a sense this sounds strange to us, doesn't it? That which is assumed as basic in this text doesn't seem all that important today. Note some assessments of the current situation.

– Reginald Bibby in *Fragmented Gods* reports that among us, ". . . religion has ceased to be life-informing at the level of the average Canadian" (Bibby: 5). Church attendance of adults is down since 1946: in 1946 two-thirds attended church, in 1986, one-third. Regarding Bible reading: 9 percent of Canadians read the Bible weekly, 4 percent daily; as a result there is little familiarity not only with the Bible but with the Christian tradition as well.

– A recent Gallup poll about Christians reported that "too many are shallow believers who fail to link religion and daily life."

– "Follow some church members through the week. Few show any signs that they are Christians. They don't read their Bibles or pray. People live lives unaffected by their faith" (*Christian Century*, May 1990).

How do these comments stack up against the assumptions and expectations of our text from Deuteronomy? The preconditions are not being met very well. There seem to be very few signs that the love of God is central in life, that the faith is part of our conversation, that it is being caringly shared with children and youth. What an indictment on us as adult believers in the church!

The text suggests a dialogical process through which the story and the faith are communicated to the next generation. The youth asks:

"What is the meaning of the ordinances and statutes?" And in response he was told the story: "We were Pharoah's slaves in Egypt . . . the Lord brought us out . . . he commanded us to do these things . . . to fear the Lord" (Deuteronomy 6:20–24).

The retelling of this story by the parents led to faith. As the children heard the story they were enabled to step into the story, to claim it as their own: "This is my story; that's the Lord in whom I believe." But that's not all that happened in the retelling. By retelling it, the father's faith was renewed and deepened. As he retold it, he relived it, and it got under his skin a bit more. The biblical narrative is the core curriculum for those already in, for those just in and for those on the way in.

The story evokes faith and it shapes life. What I mean is that the life of the story-faith teller is shaped by the telling of the story. In 1981 Eric Booth, Broadway actor recited the gospel of Mark twice a day to packed theatres in Chicago.

After the close of the program one evening, we seminary students had a chance to talk with him: "How long did you take to learn the text?"

"About five months."

"What has happened to you in the learning and telling of this gospel?"

"I find myself, my life becoming more like the life that Jesus taught about and lived." The story Booth told became a part of him; it had gotten under his skin.

When adults fail to live and tell the story, their lives fail to be shaped by it. And eventually the shaping vacuum is filled by another set of stories which receives attention and proceeds to shape life. Life will be shaped and formed by something or other, some story-line. The Christian life will be shaped by the story of the Old and New Testaments. We cannot be Christian without it. It must be kept on the front burner. Shaping means that stories support the bias of our faith; they give us our notions and models to live by. We live by stories, the stories we hear and tell.

The story shapes our self-image. Who am I before myself, God, among others? is answered in the biblical story. Through it I come to see myself as created in the image of God. Through the same story I also come to see that I am a sinner, fallen, in need of grace and forgiveness. The Hebrew youth saw himself in the story his father told him. I may not be enslaved by an Egyptian pharoah but I too might be enslaved by a modern demigod or two. I was trapped but the Lord freed me and led me into new possibilities.

In the New Testament I see myself in the crowd listening to Peter on Pentecost and I conclude: I have contributed to the crucifixion of Jesus and it was for me he prayed, "Father, forgive them; for they know not what they do" (Luke 23:34a). It is I who hear the words, "Repent and believe." I see myself in the younger son coming home with a confession of failure and sin on my lips. I see myself in the disciples' group as they hear the words, "You are my witnesses in the whole world."

Do you see what I mean? The story is the mirror in which I see myself: enslaved, redeemed, forgiven, welcomed, sent. That's me; that's who I am. The story is the lens which frees me to see what I need to know about myself in relation to God. The story cannot shape our identity unless we immerse ourselves in it. There is no other way.

The story shapes our values. This is what happened to Eric Booth. When we encounter other values and norms, the biblical story gives us guidelines, examples, intentions to live by. Through the story I learn to value persons above property which is in tension with the materialism of our time. In the story of the rich farmer, Jesus told him straight "You have your values mixed up." The story helps me unscramble my priorities. And I learn that all wealth is to be viewed as a gift, a trust from the Lord, to be used responsibly for ourselves and in generous service to others.

The story shows us that believing in and loving God must lead to helping others. This takes priority over getting ahead myself. Whenever I come across a person with a need I cannot help but think of the story of the good Samaritan. This story reminds me of the weight of prejudice under which I live in the world. Our way of dealing with persons of other backgrounds and races can be determined by an Archie Bunker value system or by the stories of Jonah, of Peter and of Jesus, who again and again broke free from their cultural limitations and erased barriers to deal caringly with others, no matter what their situation in life or their background.

By which stories will our lives be shaped? The story is the mirror in which I am invited to see myself, be changed by it. Through it I see people, things and situations in sharper focus. But again there is a condition: a casual acquaintance with the story will not lead to deeply held convictions nor will it lead to seeing, valuing and responding in Christ-like ways. The condition is immersion. If we are not drenched with the details we cannot be shaped by the story. This is the reason for regular worship, for Bible reading and study, for attending Christian schools and for continuing adult education in other settings. To grow in Christian faith, commitment and understanding, we need to become immersed in the story of God and God's people so we begin to feel, think, act and serve in ways shown in this story.

This is a personal challenge for each of us: that we do what is suggested and allow this story of God and God's people to shape us in profound ways and transform us into conformity with God's son. This is the challenge for us as churches and conferences: that we provide settings for this to be possible in addition to Sunday school, in addition to camps, in addition to weekly worship services.

The Lord will bless our commitment to this kind of life, and we will be liberated from the depressing grasshopper syndrome. If we do what is called for, we will not say that the obstacles are too great nor feel like grasshoppers. No, we will move forward as Joshua did, with these words ringing in our ears: "Be strong and of good courage, be not frightened, neither be dismayed; for the Lord your God is with you wherever you go!"

9

WITH AN EYE TO THE FUTURE

An occasion such as this is a time to celebrate the accomplishments of the past. There is much to celebrate—we as a Mennonite people have an enviable record, particularly in the field of education. Under severe pioneering conditions here in Canada, our forefathers expressed their faith and their vision by forming congregations and by building schools. To do that required sacrifice which they were prepared to make. Many of them were willing go give up getting ahead personally so that the future of our people would be assured. Such sacrifices were possible because for them church and school were given top priority. Our forefathers knew that the future depended on these.

I am thinking specifically of the emergence of RJC (Rosthern Junior College, Rosthern, Saskatchewan), of MCI (Mennonite Collegiate Institute, Gretna, Manitoba), of MEI (Mennonite Educational Institute, Clearbrook, British Columbia), of UMEI (United Mennonite Educational Institute, Leamington, Ontario), of Westgate Mennonite Collegiate (Winnipeg, Manitoba), of CMBC (Canadian Mennonite Bible College, Winnipeg) and numerous Bible schools. These private schools were brought into being—more than that, they were nurtured and developed so that their programs would be second to none—by the vision and dedication of men and women whom we know or have heard about. We cannot look to our future without looking back and recognizing that which others before us were able to do. The Lord blessed their efforts and we did not have to begin at square one. We are the recipients of a tradition and a movement.

A second fact we must recognize today—a very sobering fact—is that we are but a few short steps away from defaulting on our heritage. Unless we keep the vision alive, unless we commit our time and energy and money to our schools, we will soon be back at square one. We must realize that our schools will not be perpetually sustained by the vision of our forefathers. Unless we rethink and commit ourselves to our vision of education there will likely be no RJCs for our grandchildren.

First presented in January 1981 at a Fundraising Banquet for Rosthern Junior College, Rosthern, Saskatchewan.

As we look to the future we need to redevelop a vision that can and will be translated into moral and financial support which will be there, consistently and increasingly, even in the face of enrolment fluctuations and the ups and downs of economics. Such a sustaining vision will require more than a superficial, an on-again, off-again enthusiasm. It is necessary that we again ask the most radical questions—not "far out" but going "to the root of the matter"—questions which speak to the foundations of our faith. The dedication that our forefathers had was based on *their* radical questioning. We today must come to ownership of answers to the questions if we want to face the uncertain future with any degree of confidence and courage.

That the future is uncertain is clear to all. Change bombards us: massive hunger, poverty, arms buildup; an emphasis on individualism, on pleasure, on materialism; a society which accepts a plurality of religious views and expressions. The future we face is one in which it will be more difficult than ever before to have faith and to be faithful.

What is it that we need as we look to the future? The basic questions do not revolve around RJC or any of our school, for RJC is not an end in itself but a means to an end. Our questions must be about the church. I remind you of a statement that Jesus made to his followers, "As the Father has sent me, so I send you" (John 20:21).

The church of which you and I are members is not here to be enjoying cosy, comfortable fellowship. No, the church must never forget that she has been sent. She is on mission to the world. She is to continue to do on earth what Jesus began. He, knowing he was sent, proclaimed a new Kingdom; he turned the world upside down—personally, socially, economically, politically, religiously (Kraybill, *The Upside Down Kingdom)*. He represented a view of life and of peoplehood that was new, unheard of. We, his followers, are called to follow: "As the Father has sent me, so I send you!"

The early church believed those words. It considered itself sent and developed the structures, the dynamic, to get on with the task. Their conviction, that they were indeed sent, motivated them to come together so that they could scatter. They came together for worship, study, fellowship and instruction so that they could penetrate the various stations of their lives with the message and spirit of him who was their Lord and Saviour. *Sometimes* they came together; *often* they were scattered; *always* they were on mission.

The question they faced was: How can all believers be prepared, equipped for their ministry in the world? This is also the question I want to deal with this evening. This is the question which is basic to our understanding, our vision for our private schools.

Our churches have devised a variety of ways in which they seek to reach their goals. No one of these settings is able to do it all. The family has a crucial role to play, but families can't do it all; the church—worship and preaching—has a role to play, but it can't do it all; the Sunday school has a role to play, but the Sunday school can't do it all; our Bible schools, CMBC, Seminary have a role to play, but they can't do it all; our high schools have a role to play, but they can't do it all.

RJC is *one* of the settings which the church has created so that all believers will be more ready for their service in the world. RJC is an extension of that which we seek to do in our homes and in our churches. It has a significant role to play in the realization of four goals—which are goals of the church, not only goals of private schools.

In order that persons will continue to worship and serve Christ, our Lord and Saviour, as sent ones, we need to develop: a clear sense of identity; a sense of vocation; an awareness of issues; and the capacity to cope with crises and pressures encountered in life.

A clear sense of identity. In order for Christian believers to be involved in ministry in the world they must know who they are as persons before God and as persons among each other. That knowledge will determine our stance toward others around us.

How do we come to know who we are as believers, as members of a community of faith? The story of Israel gives us some important clues. When the Lord rescued the Israelites from Egypt, they became a people. They knew who they were, distinct from others:

> You have seen what I did to the Egyptians, and how I bore you on eagles' wings and brought you to myself. Now therefore, if you will obey my voice and keep my covenant, you shall be my own possession among all peoples; . . . you shall be to me a kingdom of priests and a holy nation (Exodus 19:4–6).

With these words they knew: they were redeemed by God; they were called to have a special purpose; they were to be a holy nation, a kingdom of priests. Everyone who trudged through the desert to Sinai had a pretty clear idea of who they were. But how would their children, yet to be born, discover who *they* were? How would this strong sense of consciousness and identity as a people be awakened in them? The question is, "How is a vision and an identity transmitted to succeeding generations?"

This was to come about when the young asked questions: "What is the meaning of these ordinances? Why? How come we do this or that?"

At that point the adults were to do some explaining (Deuteronomy 6:21–24). The children were told the story. That's how identity of the next generation is formed: by the telling and retelling of the acts of the Lord in their midst. "We live by story, by the stories constantly being told and by the stories we tell ourselves."

Basic Christian identity, like Israel's, is given and received in the story of God and God's people, reaching its peak in the story of Jesus Christ. It is through the story and through identity—shaping language—that we come to see who we are. A number of passages could be cited. Take, for example, Galatians 3:26–28. Although the host society thought racial, economic and sexual labels played a big role, Paul said that for Christians that was not to be so. Those who came to faith in Christ, came to see themselves and their relationships to God and to others on the basis of the story, told and retold, and not on the basis of the labels which society considers important. C.S. Calian writes, "Without identity, the church will be sucked into the uncertainty and relativism of our society."

RJC is a facilitator of identity, of formation and re-formation for its students. It does this through its community life, its teaching in courses, its chapel services and through special events. Out of its halls come young people who have a clearer idea of who they are as Christian believers, to which community of faith and service they belong. One more thing, RJC forges the identity of Mennonite Christians who know their heritage—who they are in distinction from believers of other denominations.

If you believe that RJC contributes to the sense of identity of our young people, that it shapes their Christian and their denominational identity, then you will support its efforts.

A sense of vocation. Not only do members of the church need to know who they are, they also need to know what for they are in the world. The question is, "What is our calling?" ("Wozu sind wir berufen?") The Bible uses many words to respond to this concern: being salt, being light, being witnesses, being ministers of reconciliation, leading lives worthy of our calling.

We can subsume this variety of expression under the term, "being sent." "God sends his people forth to do his work in the world, to live by the gospel, to offer [all] the love of Jesus Christ, to witness to his Lordship over the world. The church continues the ministry of Jesus Christ" (George Webber). This sense of vocation is the conviction that we are not only called to be in the church, we are also called to be in the world. One writer has suggested that we not only need to be converted to Christ, we also need to be converted to the world.

Whatever one's vocation, to be in the world as sent ones is most crucial. Young people coming to RJC must be exposed to the understanding that being Christian is not merely receiving Christ as Saviour and then relaxing in a well padded Boston rocker; being Christian is serving Christ and others in the traffic of daily life, be that on the farm, in business, in a profession.

The RJC setting makes a major contribution to the realization of this goal, this sense of vocation. This perspective must be present in the lives of the teachers, and it must be growing. It must be expressed in times of worship and meditation in chapels. It must be brought to the surface in classrooms and in informal contacts and conversations. It ought to be represented through invited guests.

The effect of these many efforts is cumulative. It will add up to the young persons having a view of the Christian life as a calling to serve. More than that, it will result in commitments to serve later in life. Parents and grandparents should not be surprised to find that their sons and daughters may decide to go to the ends of the earth as servants of him who was the greatest servant of all.

You know as well as I that education at RJC does and must continue to develop this sense of vocation in students. If you believe that this is a goal for our private schools and that RJC contributes to the realization of that goal, then you will support the school.

Awareness of issues. Christians who live in two overlapping worlds, the church community and the world community, need to know who they are, what for they are, and also what is going on in our world and in our churches. Jesus challenged the beliefs, practices and values which he encountered as the status quo in his world. It is incumbent on us, his followers, to also identify issues and challenge them in the name of the Lord. We must all grow in the awareness of issues that need to be confronted in church and world.

We need to be reminded that this is exactly what the early believers did. They addressed the issues of prejudice (Acts 10–11) and the relationship between cultures, socio-economic groups and the sexes (Galatians 32:8). In classes, chapels and other settings, students and teachers need to wrestle with the issues that cry for attention in our time. We in our home and local churches may not always like this, for sometimes our toes, our weaknesses, will be stepped on. But we must expect it.

If teachers in private schools cannot bring to awareness issues in church and world which are not yet being addressed in our homes and churches, then they are not doing all they should be doing. And it's not only true for those who teach Bible or ethics. These issues also intersect with science and history and literature. Previously held convictions and practices are held up for reexamination. Some views may be confirmed; in other cases students will be compelled to examine an issue for the first time; in most cases they will receive fresh insight for themselves.

The point I'm making is that if we are sent into the world, we'd better know what's going on out there! Sometimes this awareness will lead to discouragement and a sense of hopelessness. I hope our teachers will not only identify issues. I hope they will also model for our young people how they/we can live in the tension between what is and what is yet to be; that is, to live in hope.

The experience at RJC could help young people become more aware of the issues of consumption and waste of natural resources; peacemaking; materialism, advertising, covetousness; understanding of sexuality in human relationships; ethics in medicine, law, business, farming, politics; poverty, unemployment.

You and I know that RJC can and does contribute to this awareness of issues and that it, as a Christian institution, must be encouraged to do so. If you believe this to be a goal of our churches and that RJC contributes to the achieving of that goal, then you will support it.

Coping with crises. I have argued that, in order that the church be the church, four basic goals must be met, and that our private schools have a role to play in achieving those goals. Whether or not Christians will be able to serve as they ought in the world will further depend on whether they have learned to cope with crises and pressures in their own lives.

Generally speaking, crises are of two kinds: developmental and circumstantial. Developmental crises arise in connection with the normal progression of the life cycle. What we have in high school is persons in a very mixed-up period of their lives, a time of "Sturm und Drang" (storm and stress). Erik Eriksson has pointed out that in adolescence the key issue is one of identity: "Who am I? Am I accepted? Who am I in relation to my peers (of both sexes), my teachers, my parents, God?" A residential institution places these issues under a magnifying glass. There's a lot of anxiety, turmoil, anger, frustration that simply is part of being a teenager. We as parents have often stood by helplessly, not knowing what could be done. Some parents are relieved when their teens take off to live in residence and hope they emerge as a "Mensch." We need to appreciate this dimension of working with young people who are straining for independence.

The other crises are circumstantial. In a school setting these circumstances include: trouble with a roommate, being ditched by a girl/boy friend, failing an exam, having someone your age killed or die of cancer.

Whether the crises are developmental or due to circumstances, they affect what happens in classroom, in chapel, in residence and on weekends. Teachers are counsellors, confidantes and priests who, along with the students, need to develop the art of caring confrontation. Students must know that others care for them; they must also know that others will care enough to confront them with the reality of their actions, attitudes and words.

Experience at RJC should help persons in crisis know they are not alone, that they can be forgiven, that starting over is central to the Christian faith, that acceptance—not necessarily approval—is there, always. What the students can learn here is the meaning of community which listens and stands with them, so they will again be able to live life abundantly; they will again be energetic, joyful and enthusiastic.

These experiences are a resource for them not only for the time of their crisis, but also when a roommate or classmate or, later in life, a neighbour encounters pressures. Then their experience here will be something to fall back on.

If you believe that RJC has a contribution to make to the young person's ability to cope with crises and pressures, then you will support the school.

I have said that when we look to the future we must ask the most radical questions, questions which deal with the purpose of the church in the world. In order that the church be the church, believers must have a sense of identity, a sense of vocation, be aware of issues and be able to cope with crises and pressures. I have argued that RJC makes significant contributions to the achievement of these goals in the lives of its students.

The constituency, the board of directors, the faculty and staff must view their work from within the perspective that what is being done here is like sowing seed. Then comes the hoping, praying and waiting that the seed will take root, develop, ripen in the lives of young men and women, who will be better equipped for their ministry in the world.

10

AT THE INTERSECTION

[Read the book of Philemon]

While we proclaim that we are people of the Word, it has also become increasingly obvious that we are also people of the world. We are no longer isolated from the culture that surrounds us; we no longer control the influences that shape us. We are being shaped by *secularism:* living as though God were not in the picture and the attitude that in our time it is easier *not* to believe than to believe; *individualism:* every one for themselves; *pluralism:* there are many ways of looking at things, many different approaches to the truth, so you can't tell someone else what to believe; and *affluence:* having more than enough of everything material and in the process forgetting about the spiritual side of life. This is true of all believers in our culture. A few years ago several articles in Christian periodicals made this point: "Too many . . . are shallow believers who fail to link religion and daily life."

The church is not unaffected by these things. "Follow some church members through the week. Few show any signs that they are Christians. They won't read their Bibles or pray. People live lives unaffected by their faith" *(Christian Century*, May 90).

How do we bring our faith into lively dialogue with life so that we can all live the adventure of Christian pilgrimage at the intersection, there where faith, relationships and situations meet? This is the challenge we face in our homes, in our churches and in our schools.

As I pondered this reality, I remembered a short note tucked away in a corner of the New Testament: the letter of Philemon. In it we have the critical elements, a model of Christian education at its best. This letter, one of the shortest books in the New Testament, contains the words of Paul to his friend Philemon, a slave owner, about his slave Onesimus whom Paul is sending back to his master after his conversion to Christ. Some years later, the church came to the conviction that this word of one Christian to another was more than that; it was the word of God to the church.

Paul and Philemon were in a relationship that went back some years,

---

First preached in January 1995 at deeper life meetings in Leamington, Ontario.

that went beyond human social friendship. It was a relationship in which they were explicit about their common faith. They talked about the things that mattered deeply to them. They didn't just assume that they were believers and let it go at that. This relationship included praying for each other, as well as specific words of affirmation and words of hope for the future.

Look at Philemon, an adult believer, active in his house church, a deeply caring, loving person in the house fellowship in Colossae. I assume he is somewhat affluent, a slave owner, living in an urban setting. He is good to have around in church; he refreshes the hearts of the saints; he lifts their spirits. And in his daily life he assumes the naturalness of the status quo. Like the other freed men in the city, he has his slaves. He and all the other slave owners know how slaves are to be treated. He knows his rights. Life has its predictable routines and he enjoys being part of the Christian fellowship and is excited about his faith in Jesus.

One day a messenger comes to his gate with a small scroll. As he opens it he notices that it is from his friend Paul from whom he has not heard for a while. He reads on, heart aglow, because Paul mentions with appreciation his faith, his love, and that he is praying for him. Paul expresses confidence that Philemon is making a positive contribution to the fellowship. All is fine.

And then . . . Paul brings to the surface an incident out of daily life; he brings into the conversation this matter of the runaway slave, Onesimus. I take it that Philemon will have sensed a tightening of his muscles, an inner stiffening of the heart. That was life—Onesimus, his slave, had stolen and run off and he, as a slave owner, knew how to deal with runaway slaves: tie him to a post, whip him, let him die if necessary. All this was legal and expected.

But wait a minute. Paul confronts Philemon with this work-related incident and asks him to allow his Christian faith to affect his everyday life in unheard of ways. Paul simply says, "Look Philemon, I'm sending Onesimus, your runaway slave, back to you. Welcome him back as a dear brother, as you would welcome me."

Philemon is stopped in his tracks, challenged to review, rethink, reexamine, reflect on life and on faith in a new way. There is nothing suffocatingly superficial about this note from Paul. Paul has affirmed his brother's faith and compelled him to enlarge the area of life where following Jesus matters. As he ponders it, Philemon is suddenly aware that his faith has implications he had not counted on before; he is being challenged to let go of his culture's assumptions and ways and behave as a Christian in a new area of life.

I'm amazed by this note—all the elements of creative Christian education right here. In Paul we have the challenge side of Christian education. He operates on the assumption that faith matters. He confronts a fellow believer on a faith-practice issue, risking even the loss of the relationship. He exerts authoritative theological pressure but in a dialogical, relationship-based way.

In Philemon we have the experience side of education. He stands at the point of intersection where faith and life and relationships all meet. And there he is pushed or lured or prodded to examine a part of his status quo on the basis of his faith in Christ.

In the coming together of these two—Paul's note and Philemon's critical moment—there is relationship, affirmation, prayer, expanded awareness; and there is a new frightening insight: there is a decision to be made. There is the possibility of enlarged commitment. This is a moment of Christian education at its best.

In creative Christian education, four elements are crucial:

Relationships are critical—in our families, classes, groups, church meetings, work places. On the basis of relationships there can be affirmation, challenge, even personal confrontation.

Explicit faith is needed. Paul is not hesitant about saying what they both knew and what they simply might have assumed. Over 20 years ago, I accompanied a youth leadership group for a weekend retreat. As we looked over the program, I noticed they had scheduled no time for worship, Bible study or devotions. I asked the leader. "Oh," he said, "we assume that." Paul would not assume faith. He talked about it.

Real life, our daily work situation, is co-curriculum in Christian education. Actual experiences, dilemmas are brought into conversation with the faith. The faith measures and judges them. We must know the faith well and we must be open to reflect on our experiences in the light of that faith.

Creative Christian education includes both wholehearted affirmation and encouragement as well as risky confrontation and frightening challenges.

If we allow Philemon, this little note from Paul, to be our model for Christian education, we will not remain shallow believers; we will not sideline scripture; we will not ignore daily situations and dilemmas. However, if we dare to take this note seriously, then our faith will have a life-transforming, dramatic impact on our lives.

I hope all of us will dare to live at this intersection, where explicit faith, relationships and daily experiences meet. At such an intersection we have the possibility of growth and faithfulness.

11

LIVING IN AN ELLIPSE

They devoted themselves to the apostles' teaching and fellowship, to the breaking of bread and the prayers. Awe came upon everyone because many wonders and signs were being done by the apostles. All who believed were together and had all things in common; they would sell their possessions and goods and distribute the proceeds to all, as any had need. Day by day, as they spent much time together in the temple, they broke bread at home and ate their food with glad and generous hearts, praising God and having the goodwill of all the people. And day by day the Lord added to their number those who were being saved (Acts 2:42–47).

The gifts he gave were that some would be apostles, some prophets, some evangelists, some pastors and teachers, to equip the saints for the work of ministry, for building up the body of Christ, until all of us come to the unity of the faith and of the knowledge of the Son of God, to maturity, to the measure of the full stature of Christ. We must no longer be children, tossed to and fro and blown about by every wind of doctrine, by people's trickery, by their craftiness in deceitful scheming. But speaking the truth in love, we must grow up in every way into him who is the head, into Christ, from whom the whole body, joined and knit together by every ligament with which it is equipped, as each part is working properly, promote the body's growth in building itself up in love (Ephesians 4:11–16).

In many ways your life and mine are quite different—we have different life experiences, different stories to tell. But one of the things we all share, no matter what the details of our lives are, is that we are all part of the Christian church. That is very important because the church is the only body on earth that concerns itself with keeping alive the memory of Jesus in the world. No one and nothing else on earth does that.

First preached in June 1989 at First Mennonite Church, Saskatoon, Sask.

However, the church, important as it is, does not need our unthinking allegiance. The church needs loving critics who are willing to ask the hard questions, questions which lead in the direction of greater faithfulness and relevance. I will use the analogy of an ellipse to help us think about what it means to be the church in our time.

The church, worldwide, and the Mennonite church, embraces and affirms an amazing variety in languages, cultures and worship practices. But all God's people also have a great deal in common. We share the same story which reached its peak in the coming of Jesus; we share the same scriptures as our faithful guide in matters of faith and life; we share the same hope of God's kingdom being realized more and more in people's lives; and we all live in an ellipse.

Let me explain what I mean. This is not a biblical analogy, but it captures a fundamental biblical truth about the church. The ellipse with its two foci reminds us that as individual believers and as congregations, we live sometimes gathered and often gathered. Those are the two poles of our Christian existence: we gather sometimes, we scatter often. This is what the people of God—the church—habitually do: they gather and they scatter, repeatedly, consciously.

When we as Christians gather, we come together for worship, prayer, hearing God's Word, singing, fellowship, and for leaning on each other. When we as Christians scatter, we go to our places of work, our residences and our social and recreational involvements. When we gather we affirm our faith and our commitment to Jesus as Lord and Saviour. When we scatter we seek to live out our confession by being witnesses, by being salt and light in our communities and among the people we meet.

Mark talks about Jesus and his disciples in this way (3:14): that they might be with him and that he might send them out. What I see here is the ellipse without the ellipse language: to be with him (gathering) and to be sent out (scattering).

Another way of saying this is that we need to experience a double conversion. We need to be converted to be with Christ and to be with other believers. We accept Jesus as giving us three things: forgiveness of sin, guidance for life and a people to belong to. All of these come together when we gather, as the Acts passage says, "They devoted themselves to the apostles' teaching and fellowship, to the breaking of bread and the prayers. . . . All who believed were together and had all things in common. . . . They spent much time together" (2:42,44–45).

I wonder when they found time for daily work: jobs, children, housekeeping, farming.These people were converted to Christ and to each other, but if that was all, their life would be lopsided and ineffective. It would have been too cosy, too much of an in-group, even cliquish. As believers they needed to be moved to the other pole, to be converted not only to Christ and his body but to the world. They needed to hear the second thing Mark talked about: that they were called not only to be together with Christ; they were also called to be sent out. They needed to learn and to affirm the scattering. They needed to see as very important that part of their Christian experience which took them away from the gathered body and scattered them to their places of work, residence and social life—not grudgingly, but with joy and enthusiasm. The light needs to shine; the salt needs to get out of the salt shaker; the witness needs to be given by word and deed among those who have not yet heard the good news.

Let me tell a story. Some time ago I preached a sermon in which I used Philemon as a text. I made the point that what Paul urged Philemon as a Christian to do was to give Onesimus, a runaway slave, a second chance at his place of work. Two weeks after that sermon a woman from our church, who was a forelady in a dry cleaning place, came to the office and said, "John, I did it!"

"What are you talking about?" I asked.

Her reply, "I did your sermon . . ."

I want to emphasize that we need a balance between the gathering and the scattering. We cannot and should not always be together as a body of believers. We need time to relate to our neighbours—loving and caring takes time. We cannot always be involved with others either. We do need time away from meeting others' needs. There is a time for withdrawal and renewal so that we can serve others with enthusiasm.

In other words, there should be a rhythm in our lives, sometimes gathering, often scattering. And the rhythm of moving from one pole to the other links two things which must be held together. Note the text from Ephesians 4. When we gather, we are built up as a body and we are equipped for service. The text says that in the church there will be apostles, prophets, evangelists, pastors and teachers whose role is concentrated on the gathered church. Their responsibility is to build up the body and to prepare God's people for works of service. The ministry and service of "the many" is not primarily carried out on Sunday morning. The ministry of most believers is done in the context of their homes, their work, their social and recreational life.

This is the vital link between gathering and scattering, between worship and work, between faith and life. The agenda of our worship time must intersect with the agenda of our work and leisure time. When we come together for worship, we bring the issues of daily life with us—they are not left in the parking place. When we scatter, we bring with us the faith we have professed together with others. It's like a song says, "Worship and work must be one."

The Ephesians text raises one more question: What would a person equipped for service be like? What are the distinguishing marks of someone who lives in the ellipse and moves rhythmically from scattered to gathered, from gathered to scattered? Our text doesn't tell us the answer, but I would suggest four marks of a person who is learning to live in the ellipse. Such persons will have: a growing sense of Christian and denominational identity; a sense of call to serve; an increasing awareness of issues needing attention; and a growing capacity to cope with crises and pressures.

Let us examine the rhythm of our lives—whether we are in motion—sometimes gathering, often scattering. Let us recommit ourselves to Christ and the brothers and sisters who gather and to the neighbour with a cluster of needs. Let us commit ourselves to being equipped so that we can serve our Lord and his people, whether we gather or scatter.

12

ON BEING LEADERS—CONSIDER MOSES

Then [God] said, "Come no closer! Remove the sandals from your feet, for the place on which you are standing is holy ground." He said further, "I am the God of your father, the God of Abraham, the God of Isaac, and the God of Jacob." And Moses hid his face, for he was afraid to look at God. Then the Lord said, "I have observed the misery of my people who are in Egypt; I have heard their cry on account of their taskmasters. Indeed, I know their sufferings, and I have come down to deliver them from the Egyptians, and to bring them up out of that land to a good and broad land, a land flowing with milk and honey, to the country of the Canaanites, the Hittites, the Amorites, the Perizzites, the Hivites, and the Jebusites. The cry of the Israelites has now come to me; I have also seen how the Egyptians oppress them. So come, I will send you to Pharaoh to bring my people, the Israelites, out of Egypt" (Exodus 3:5–10).

In recent months I have heard it said in one way or another that we are in fact living in a time of crisis. Certainly there are crises on the international scene; there are crises on the domestic scene: the lingering recession, unemployment, etc.; and there are crises in our personal and family lives and in our churches and in the conferences. At a meeting in Chicago in December Edgar Stoesz said, "We have a tired constituency which has lost its missionary program. . . . We also have tired programs."

What I mean by crisis is that we are facing challenges on a number of fronts: in being faithful in evangelism and outreach; in stewardship of our wealth—dealing with the tension between "conspicuous consumption" and "conspicuous contentment" (Christian Smith, *Going to the Root*); in meeting our budgets; in finding the resources to realize our dreams and our visions in our various ministries and in our Conference program.

First preached in February 1993 at opening worship for Council of Boards of the Conference of Mennonites in Canada.

Crises are one of the givens; the other given is leaders. You and I are leaders, each in our own settings; then we have been called by our constituency to be leaders together for our people. In order to be faithful in dealing with the challenges we face as a church in our time, we will need to give further attention to effective Christian leadership. Let us consider Moses as a paradigmatic leader, as a model for our leadership.

There are some interesting parallels between his time and ours, between his role and ours. He, like we, was called to lead in a time of crisis. Did you notice the crisis language in the text: affliction, cry, sufferings? And right on the heels of all this crisis language, the call, "Come, I will send you to Pharoah that you may bring forth my people out of Egypt" (v.10). Depending on the decisions the people would make under his leadership, they would either move forward in the direction of redemption and responsibility as the people of God, or they could sink deeper and deeper into bondage, hopelessness and despair.

Moses was called to lead in a time of competing faith systems, and the two dominant faiths could not be harmonized. Never. One could not have it both ways. Either Pharaoh was lord or Yahweh was Lord. The good news of the possibility of redemption had to be voiced and heard in the public sphere—in open competition with the views of the dominant culture. We too are called to proclaim the gospel in settings in which other ideologies, other faiths and different convictions compete for the hearts and minds and souls of the very same people we are called to serve. That is a critical situation, a situation of heightened vulnerability and/or potential.

Moses came to leadership with his basketful of earlier experiences; and for him those life experiences were both promises and threats, the basis of encouragement as well as discouragement for the leadership role he was to assume. On the positive side, his secular education and training in Pharaoh's court provided him with a set of tools for easy communication later on. He knew how their system worked from the inside; he knew what the operating assumptions of the Egyptians were. His experience in the desert of Midian provided him with a set of learnings which would come in handy as he led his people across the barren dunes. Other things in his past were negative and hindered his leadership—in his early years he did a rash, unwise thing in an attempt to help. His good intentions were poorly expressed and he had to flee with a murder rap on his head. Certainly that was not an asset as he returned to the court of Pharoah. We too bring baskets full of experience to our leadership functions. Some of them are definite assets for leadership; others may well be decided hindrances for leadership.

Moses received a call to leadership while engaged in his life's work. Responding to that call meant making a radical career change. When the call came, he was certainly reminded of earlier attempts to help, attempts which had failed. And he could give his list of excuses: "Lord, how could I go and do this? If I go, who shall I say sent me? And what if they don't believe, what then? And Lord, don't send me; you see, I'm not good at public speaking. Please Lord, send someone else."

My hunch is that when we face critical decisions at home or in our conference work, we can easily identify with Moses in making excuses and saying why it would be better if the Lord called someone else to do the work, to make the tough decisions. But the Lord effectively told Moses to shut his mouth and listen: "I am calling you and I will be with you. Now get on with it!"

Moses, the poor speaker, became the proclaimer of God's message in two arenas: the arena of God's people and the public arena of Pharaoh's court. At its core the message was simple: Yahweh is Lord, not Pharaoh the competitor god nor the oppressive status quo. With this message Moses became both an evangelist and a social activist. As evangelist, he invited the people to faith and commitment; as social activist, he challenged the oppressive system sustained by Pharaoh. Moses' message was relevant to both audiences. He spoke in ways that the people knew, "This man knows our situation from the inside. He's offering us an exit, a new life, hope." They understood him, and they were compelled to make decisions, to believe or not to believe.

We as leaders are also proclaimers. Has our message been as unambiguous as Moses'? Has our message been evangelistic in the sense that Moses' was, linking the message of hope and good news with the very real bondage the people knew? Has our message been broad and deep enough to speak to the systems in our society which are committed to perpetuating the status quo? Have those who oppress and exploit and abuse heard the claim that Yahweh is Lord?

In spite of his protestations Moses became a leader. Sometimes he stood alone, at other times he stood in partnership with Aaron and Miriam and the 70 elders. As a leader he received criticism from his own people, from the power brokers and from his father-in-law. It was his father-in-law who warned him about burn-out and pointed to the strategy of delegation in order to do more by doing less. Sometimes he showed flexibility, sometimes inflexibility. In relation to Pharaoh, Moses showed the capacity and courage to be assertive, to insist, and not to back down. In both the arenas in which he exercised leadership Moses was larger than life.

Even if we have tried to fight off leadership, each of us has become a leader. And we lead, at times effectively, at other times less effectively than we would like. Are we able when necessary to envision, to implement, to do things in partnership with others and if necessary, even alone? And are we ready for criticism? Are we teachable to try new ways of doing things? Can we discern when it's best to remain assertive and to stand our ground?

Moses as leader was the celebrant of ritual, a priest and a teacher. The message he spoke was enacted in ritual—the passover, the covenant-sealing ceremony. He acted as mediator priest, interceding for his people when they had sinned. As mediator he stood with and alongside his people. He was a teacher—reviewing, repeating and reinterpreting the Word of God for the people.

We as leaders can stand with the people we serve as Moses did again and again, or we can stand separate and apart. We as leaders can represent the people in their praising and petitioning of God. We as leaders have the opportunity of carefully teaching the whole counsel of God to our people. Will we accept the challenge and take the opportunities as Moses did?

I am suggesting that we as leaders need to look into the mirror of God's Word and find there the paradigms for evaluating our leading. God certainly offers a challenge to each of us in our separate roles and to all of us together as leaders within our Conference and its institutions.

One final thing, the Lord used Moses, the fully human one, the richly gifted one, the tragically flawed one, to accomplish salvation, liberation and hope for his people. Certainly God will continue to use each of us and all of us together, flawed as we may be, to God's glory. Like Moses we have this treasure, the gospel of Jesus Christ, in earthen vessels, in order to show that "the supreme power belongs to God, and not to us" (2 Corinthians 4:7).

Church Year
and
Special Occasions

13

BLESSED MARY AND HER WORDS

In the sixth month the angel Gabriel was sent by God to a town in Galilee called Nazareth, to a virgin engaged to a man whose name was Joseph, of the house of David. The virgin's name was Mary. And he came to her and said, "Greetings, favoured one! The Lord is with you." But she was much perplexed by his words and pondered what sort of greeting this might be. The angel said to her, "Do not be afraid, Mary, for you have found favour with God. And now, you will conceive in your womb and bear a son, and you will name him Jesus. He will be great, and will be called the Son of the Most High, and the Lord God will give to him the throne of his ancestor David. He will reign over the house of Jacob forever, and of his kingdom there will be no end." Mary said to the angel, "How can this be, since I am a virgin?" The angel said to her, "The Holy Spirit will come upon you, and the power of the Most High will overshadow you; therefore the child to be born will be holy; he will be called Son of God. And now, your relative Elizabeth in her old age has also conceived a son; and this is the sixth month for her who was said to be barren. For nothing will be impossible with God." Then Mary said, "Here am I, the servant of the Lord; let it be with me according to your word." Then the angel departed from her. . . .

And Mary said, "My soul magnifies the Lord, and my spirit rejoices in God my Saviour, for he has looked with favour on the lowliness of his servant.

"Surely, from now on all generations will call me blessed; for the Mighty One has done great things for me, and holy is his name. His mercy is for those who fear him from generation to generation.

"He has shown strength with his arm; he has scattered the proud in the thoughts of their hearts. He has brought down the powerful from their thrones, and lifted up the lowly; he has filled

---

First preached in December 1991 at First Mennonite Church, Winnipeg, Manitoba.

the hungry with good things, and sent the rich away empty. He has helped his servant Israel, in remembrance of his mercy, according to the promise he made to our ancestors, to Abraham and to his descendants forever" (Luke 1:26–38, 46–55).

Before we consider the two texts about Mary, let me make three comments. Some years ago when I was working with these passages about Mary, a Mennonite biblical scholar encouraged me with the words, "It's about time." What David Schroeder was referring to was the fact that Mennonites and Protestants generally have avoided preaching on Mary. Catholics have a strong tradition surrounding Mary: She is blessed Mary, mother of God, herself immaculately conceived. Our text does not point very far in that direction. Mary is presented by Luke as very human, a person aware that God took the initiative to come to her; God extended mercy and a special role to her. Certainly she is "Blessed Mary"—the words are in the text—but we haven't paid much attention to her except in Christmas carols and some choir anthems.

My second comment is about us and how we use language. During the Christmas season we use two kinds of language in our conversations: there's "general talk" about the Christmas season, talk that's accessible to everyone in society, believers as well as unbelievers. Then there's "insider talk" which is at home in Christian circles, where the meaning of Christmas as a Christian celebration is central.

The story is told of a woman who was selecting carols to be used at a community Christmas tree lighting. She looked at the options and complained, "Most of the Christmas songs are too distressingly theological."

The person on the other side of the counter said, "But after all, Christmas is a rather theological affair."

That's the difference. The woman was looking for Xmas carols where the X is undefined. Insiders know that the X in Xmas is the first letter in Greek for "Xristos." In this sermon we will use "insider talk" and delve into the meanings beneath the events that we Christians celebrate at Christmas.

My third comment is connected with an experience I had on December 6. It was Friday, the 100th anniversary of the burial of Mozart. On that day, Bramwell Tovey, conductor of the Winnipeg Symphony Orchestra, came to speak in the chapel service at CMBC. Tovey is not only a fine conductor; he is also an excellent speaker. He showed how Mozart used several basic chords to create an incredible range of music. I've enjoyed Mozart's music for a long time but didn't know how it was put together. Tovey's talk and demonstration on the piano were an eye opener for me.

You may well be wondering what all this has to do with Mary and her words. The point I want to make is that Luke is a literary artist as Mozart was a musical artist. When we probe these texts, we actually find more than meets the eye on a quick reading. The more we examine these words, the closer we get to what Luke was trying to communicate to his readers. Luke, the physician and writer, draws on expressions, themes and memories from the circle of insiders and weaves them into a masterful story. He is a literary artist who uses the story we know to say more than it says.

Let us look at the annunciation story, but not only as a private and personal story. Mary is who she is, but for Luke she is also a prototype, a model of a true Christian. She speaks for the people of God and expresses the faith of the church. If Luke had wanted to treat Mary simply as Mary, he would have dealt with different things: How and when did this teenage girl tell her parents that she was expecting? How did she deal with the dilemma of telling Joseph, her betrothed, that she was an expecting virgin? Would he believe her? Get angry? Reject her? And what about the talk and gossip in Nazareth about this teenager, now mysteriously pregnant?

Luke says nothing, not a word, not even a hint about any of this. It did not suit his purpose. He sees Mary as the representative of the people of God—incidentally, she's a woman! Through her believing response to the angel's word, Luke expresses the hopes and longing and the believing of the people. The expressions he uses reach back into the collective memory of Israel, all the way back to Abraham. And when Mary speaks (before the child is born), she hints at what will happen with the grown Jesus and at what the church would come to believe about him after Pentecost.

Let's look at some of the details of Luke 1:26–38. Why is Mary perplexed at the angel's greeting? "Greetings, favoured one! The Lord is with you." She is a woman being addressed by a male (albeit an angel), a surprise in her culture. She is told, "*You* have found favour with God." As a woman Mary was aware that there were limits and boundaries. She did not have access to the temple nor the synagogue. Only Jewish males were permitted and admitted in the inner circle. Women and Gentiles were kept away from the centre of things with an area on the periphery being reserved for them. Now Mary hears these amazing words: you, a woman, "have found favour with God." It may be worth noting that the birth of John was announced to Zechariah, the father, not Elizabeth, his wife who would conceive in her old age.

The message Mary receives is simple, "You will conceive in your womb and bear a son."

Her response, "How can this be, since I am a virgin?"

Gabriel's answer, "The Holy Spirit will come upon you," and the sign will be that "your relative Elizabeth in her old age has also conceived a son."

At the end of the story, we read the words, "For nothing will be impossible with God." These are the kinds of words we expect in the Bible. But Luke isn't only using "easy words." These words are a link to the past, a reaching back to the story of Abram and Sarah. They too were given a promise with the words, "Nothing will be impossible with God."

The new initiative by the Lord is linked with that previous undertaking when God called the people—in Abraham. In this way Luke declares that Mary will be to the new Israel, the church, what Abraham was to the old Israel. Once Abraham was challenged to believe God's promise; now Mary is challenged to believe God's action and be part of God's new beginning. Together with Mary, you and I are invited to hear the Word of God, believe it and obey.

Earlier I said that Mary was the model believer, one for whom the Word was enough. She surrendered to the risk and the promise and became the prototype of all believers. And it was risky. She risked shame and misunderstanding: from her family, from neighbours and from Joseph. She risked going through life with a damaged reputation. With her believing, obedient response, Mary continues to challenge each of us. When and where are we ready to do what she did when she declared, "Here am I, the servant of the Lord; let it be with me according to your word?"

In this encounter between Gabriel and young Mary, we also learn a bit about who the babe will be: "You will name him Jesus. . . . He will be great, and will be called the Son of the Most High, and the Lord God will give to him the throne of the house of Jacob forever, and of his kingdom there will be no end" (1:32–33). Here are more links with the faith of Israel and the hope of Israel, for a messiah-liberator who would come. Here there is an echo of ancient prophecies lodged in the memory of the people.

But these are not only echoes from the past, but also hints of the future. These words anticipate what the voice will say at Jesus' baptism: "You are my Son, the Beloved; with you I am well pleased" (Luke

3:22b), and what the centurion will say at the foot of the cross, "Truly, this man was God's Son!" (Matthew 27:54b). And between his baptism and death, the grown Jesus declared, "The kingdom of God has come near; repent, and believe in the good news."

Luke has introduced some of the key themes of Jesus' life and work—and with them the invitation to submit to God's reign, God's new initiative, as Mary did. For one day every knee shall bow and every tongue confess that Jesus Christ is Lord.

In the meeting of the two mothers-to-be, the old woman Elizabeth and the teenaged Mary (Luke 1:39–45), the words, "Blessed are you," are heard twice. Mary's response to the blessing-word from Elizabeth is found in the Magnificat (1:46–55). These word carry a message, a challenge, to every generation. E. Stanley Jones has called this "the most revolutionary document of the world."

The song of praise divides into two parts. The first is praise for God's mighty act for one woman: "My soul magnifies the Lord, and my spirit rejoices in God my Saviour, for he has looked with favour on the lowliness of his servant. . . . The Mighty One has done great things for me, and holy is his name."

The second half has a broader concern. Not one woman but all people are invited to be part of the Lord's social revolution when God turns things upside down and right side up. What Mary herself experienced—that she, a simple, unassuming woman was receiving the unheard of privilege of bearing the Messiah—becomes the sign for God's action in the world. In the one small event the greater event, an ongoing one, is hidden.

Here is Mary's manifesto, and the faith of the church which received God's mercy: an undeserved favour is a sign, a pointer, that the Lord intends to exalt other lowly persons. That is what God is up to in the world. All who fear him, receive the gift of mercy, from generation to generation; but those who think they have some claim to God, they shall be scattered. The child who is introduced as ruler dethrones all those who exercise power. He lifts high the lowly as he lifted Mary. The rich who rely on their wealth for status and rank are sent packing, empty handed. The hungry are filled with good things. Mary's song sings of one reversal after another. That which we thought counted and mattered does not count and matters little. This is what God is up to in the birth of Jesus.

Remember the parable which Jesus told about two men going to pray. One was a Pharisee who had it all: reputation, rank, social standing; the other was a publican, despised by the respectable. The

Pharisee was smug and secure, sure of God's favour. Certainly God would take note of his accomplishments and his record—that's how he stood before God that day. The publican, with bowed head, stood at the back, softly, timidly saying, "Lord, be merciful to me, a sinner."

This parable, as does Mary's song, turns the tables. The humble publican who seemingly had no chance leaves justified; while the self-confident, self-righteous Pharisee leaves empty. Like Mary, the publican receives the blessing, God's mercy. That's what our text is all about: Mary experienced what Jesus later taught and what the church continues to teach, also at Advent.

The Christian celebration of Christmas calls each of us, younger or older, to give up pride, to relinquish power, to hang loose with our wealth, and let the Babe be conceived and be born again—in your life and in mine.

14

EATING WITH SINNERS

*One of the Pharisees asked Jesus to eat with him, and he went
into the Pharisee's house and took his place at the table. And a
woman in the city, who was a sinner, having learned that he was
eating in the Pharisee's house, brought an alabaster jar of
ointment. She stood behind him at his feet, weeping, and began
to bathe his feet with her tears and to dry them with her hair.
Then she continued kissing his feet and anointed them with the
ointment. Now when the Pharisee who had invited him saw it, he
said to himself, "If this man were a prophet, he would have
known who and what kind of woman this is who is touching
him—that she is a sinner." Jesus spoke up and said to him,
"Simon, I have something to say to you." "Teacher," he replied,
"Speak." "A certain creditor had two debtors; one owed five
hundred denarii, and the other fifty. When they could not pay, he
cancelled the debts for both of them. Now which of them will love
him more?" Simon answered, "I suppose the one for whom he
cancelled the greater debt." And Jesus said to him, "You have
judged rightly." Then turning toward the woman, he said to
Simon, "Do you see this woman? I entered your house; you gave
me no water for my feet, but she has bathed my feet with her tears
and wiped them with her hair. You gave me no kiss, but from the
time I came in she has not stopped kissing my feet. You did not
anoint my head with oil, but she has anointed my feet with
ointment. Therefore, I tell you, her sins, which were many, have
been forgiven; hence she has shown great love. But the one to
whom little is forgiven little, loves little." Then he said to her,
"Your sins are forgiven." But those who were at the table with
him began to say among themselves, "Who is this who even
forgives sins?" And he said to the woman, "Your faith has saved
you; go in peace"* (Luke 7:36–50).

First preached in March 1969 at Albright United Methodist Church, Elkhart,
Indiana.

This passage stands uniquely among the gospels. Except for the story of the healing of the paralytic (Matthew 9, Mark 2, Luke 5), it is the only gospel account in which the words, "Your sins are forgiven" occur. In Luke it stands after the comment that Jesus was "a glutton and a drunkard, a friend of tax collectors and sinners" (7:34). This story is a vivid example of why Jesus won such a bad reputation. The incident is packed with dramatic emotion. With whom do you identify in this story: Simon or the woman?

Simon, the Pharisee extends an honour to Jesus by inviting him over for dinner. Jesus accepts and goes to eat with him. While they recline at the low tables, half sitting, half lying, with their bare feet stretched out behind them away from the table, a woman, known in town as an immoral woman, enters the room. This in itself was not out of the ordinary—the doors would have been wide open and beggars and others could come in, and so could this woman.

She pays attention to no one else, but kneels on the floor at Jesus' feet, weeping so that her tears wet his feet. Then she loosens her long hair—which a decent woman would not do in that day—and dries his feet with her hair. Then, of all things, she kisses Jesus' feet and perfumes them with a flask of myrrh which she had brought with her.

Three times in our passage Luke draws attention to the fact that this woman was "a sinner." Jesus pays no attention to her, but goes on with his meal. But he did pay a lot of attention to Simon, his host, and Simon was doing a lot of hard thinking about Jesus.

Simon, a Pharisee, could not defile himself through contact with a woman of such bad reputation. He has invited Rabbi Jesus, assuming that he was a prophet. But as Jesus permits this woman to express herself in this emotional way, he thinks to himself, "If this man were a prophet, he would know what sort of woman is touching him, for she is a sinner."

This sets the stage for the real drama of the story. There sits the host, Simon. And his guest, Jesus. And there is the woman. She has expressed deep emotion. Simon is burning with contempt and anger toward the woman and with deep suspicion against Jesus. But Jesus in the middle seems to be calm, ready to work with this hot situation. He confronts these two sinners: one self-righteous, respectable; the other broken-hearted, repentant.

Simon thought Jesus was a prophet, one who ought to have a higher level of insight into people, but he begins to change his mind when he notices the woman. She is the one who focuses the tension between Simon and Jesus. Simon asks "what sort" of woman she is. He classifies people, pigeonholes them. All people are put into neat categories. She belongs to the class, "sinners," and since he already has her labelled he knows exactly how to relate to her. Sinners means no contact, contempt, disdain, defilement.

Simon thought Jesus also worked with classes of people, but Jesus didn't. Jesus turns to the woman and says to Simon, "Do you know *this* woman?" Jesus did not ask what sort of woman she was, but asked who she is.

Simon had also pigeonholed Jesus: prophet. And he knew what to expect of prophets. He thought he knew how prophets ought to know people and how they should recoil from contact with such vile sinners. But as Jesus permits this woman to wash and dry and perfume his feet, Simon re-categorizes Jesus. He assumes he must be ignorant.

Are we more like Simon or like Jesus? Do we pigeonhole, label and judge persons by groups? Hillbillies: oh, they're hillbillies and we know what to expect of them and how to relate to them. Negroes: they're all that way; you can't trust them. We label someone and we think we know how to handle them all. But Jesus did not work that way: he did not treat Pharisees that way, for example, Nicodemus; he did not treat Samaritans that way, for example, the woman at the well; he did not treat sinners and publicans that way, for example, Matthew.

Simon thought Jesus had little insight into the woman, but Jesus goes on to show that he has very deep insight not only into the woman's heart but also into Simon's heart. He demonstrates this by telling the parable of the two debtors (7:41–42).

Then Jesus turns to the woman and says to Simon, "Do you see (know) this woman? I entered your house, *you* gave me no water for my feet, but *she* has wet my feet with her tears and wiped them with her hair. *You* gave me no kiss, but . . . *she* has not ceased to kiss my feet. *You* did not anoint my head with oil, but *she* has anointed my feet with ointment" (v. 44–45).

With the parable and the pointed application, Jesus has shown rare insight into the human heart: the woman's and Simon's. Jesus says to Simon, "Look, this woman's action which you hold in contempt is proof that she has been forgiven much. In effect, Simon, your lack of action shows that you have not been forgiven much—if at all."

Jesus teaches that when a person is forgiven he or she feels like expressing gratitude and love. Simon thought he was better off than the woman: he has lived such a good clean life; he is proud of his record. He has not sensed his own deep need of forgiveness from God.

The woman has been living under the damning judgement of the

Law. Her kind of life was miserably wrong. She had gone from day to day feeling the accusing eyes of her good neighbours. How could she undo the things she had done? How shall her life be mended? How could her guilt be removed?

Simon accuses her, not realizing that something big has happened. She has experienced the healing forgiveness of Jesus in her life. Her world is now new. She has repented. She is cutting herself free from those things in her past which seek her destruction and denying their power over her. She has been forgiven, allowing the past to lose its sting and its curse, freeing her for joyful gratitude, joyful living and service in spite of failures in her past. Being forgiven prompted a sacrifice from her.

Simon's problem is that he has not realized the extent of his own sin. He has been so preoccupied with the sins of others. He is like the elder son in the Luke 15 parable. The younger son "came to himself" and entered deeply into forgiveness and the experience of sonship. The elder son, like Simon, never "came to himself" and forfeited forgiveness.

The difference between the woman and Simon was not that she was such a bad sinner, but that she realized more deeply than he the reality of her own sin. Jesus says that her love proves her forgiven. Then, so that she would never forget the experience, he says to her, "Your sins are forgiven. You are free from your past, free to live with me."

During this Lenten season, we look in the mirror of Luke's story—and we see ourselves: either as Simon or as the woman. Jesus calls us to experience his forgiveness on earth and to sacrifice out of gratitude to him.

15

A FATHER AND TWO SONS

*Now all the tax collectors and sinners were coming near to listen
to him. and the Pharisees and the scribes were grumbling and
saying, "This fellows welcomes sinners and eats with them." So
he told them this parable: . . . "There was a man who had two
sons. The younger of them said to his father, 'Father, give me the
share of the property that will belong to me.' So he divided his
property between them. A few days later the younger son
gathered all he had and travelled to a distant country, and there
he squandered his property in dissolute living. When he had
spent everything, a severe famine took place throughout that
country, and he began to be in need. So he went and hired
himself out to one of the citizens of that country, who sent him to
his fields to feed the pigs. He would gladly have filled himself
with the pods that the pigs were eating; and no one gave him
anything. But when he came to himself he said, 'How many of my
father's hired hand have bread enough and to spare, but here I
am dying of hunger! I will get up and go to my father and I will
say to him, "Father, I have sinned against heaven and before
you; I am no longer worthy to be called your son; treat me like
one of your hired hands."' So he set off and went to his father.
But while he was still far off, his father saw him and was filled
with compassion; he ran and put his arms around him and kissed
him. Then the son said to him, 'Father, I have sinned against
heaven and before you; I am no longer worthy to be called your
son.' But the father said to his slaves, 'Quickly, bring out a
robe—the best one—and put it on him; put a ring on his finger
and sandals on his feet. And get the fatted calf and kill it, and let
us eat and celebrate; for this son of mine was dead and is alive
again; he was lost and is found!' And they began to celebrate.
"Now his elder son was in the field; and when he came and*

Preached in April 1995 at a chapel service at Westgate Mennonite Collegiate,
Winnipeg, Manitoba; adapted from a sermon first preached in March 1995 at
First Mennonite Church, Winnipeg.

approached the house, he heard music and dancing. He called one of the slaves and asked what was going on. He replied, 'Your brother has come, and your father has killed the fatted calf, because he has got him back safe and sound.' Then he became angry and refused to go in. His father came out and began to plead with him. But he answered his father, 'Listen! For all these years I have been working like a slave for you, and I have never disobeyed your command; yet you have never given me even a young goat so that I might celebrate with my friends. But when this son of yours came back, who has devoured your property with prostitutes, you killed the fatted calf for him!' Then the father said to him, 'Son, you are always with me, and all that is mine is yours. But we had to celebrate and rejoice, because this brother of yours was dead and has come to life; he was lost and has been found'" (Luke 15:1–3, 11–32).

For twenty years Kenneth Bailey lived in the Middle East, teaching and researching the New Testament. One thing he was trying to find out was what impact the culture of the storyteller and the original listeners might have had on understanding the seemingly simple parables in the New Testament. He spent days and weeks in remote villages, villages which had hardly changed since the first century. He took the parables of Jesus back to the villagers who lived in an oral rather than a print culture and retold them, inviting the villagers to share their understandings of what Jesus meant.

Let us consider one parable, the story of the prodigal son, through the eyes of Kenneth Bailey. To do so will reveal what you and I are like; it will also show what God is like in relation to us—both of these are key concerns during the Lenten period.

The setting. The story begins in an atmosphere of confrontation and criticism (Luke 15:1–2). Jesus is charged publicly by the Pharisees that he is "receiving sinners"—really welcoming them, enjoying his time with them. Pharisees were particularly upset that he sits at table with them and eats with them. The Pharisees work in the crowd, behind the scenes and create an undercurrent of discontent and criticism. What does Jesus do when he becomes aware of this? Does he lash out at them? Does he change his ways? Does he leave the scene?

No, he treats them with dignity; he takes the time to tell his critics a story, luring them onto the stage where the drama is being played. You and I are invited onto the stage too, to stand with the tax collectors, the sinners and the Pharisees, to listen, more than to listen. We are invited to become part of this drama.

A father and his two sons. There was a man who had two sons. As we shall see, one known by what he did; the other by what he did *not* do.

One day the younger of them said to his father, "Father, give me the share of the property that will belong to me after you die. Give it to me now. I can't wait until you die."

Fifteen years ago Kenneth Bailey talked to villagers in the Middle East and asked them: Has anyone ever made such a request in your village? Never! Could anyone ever make such a request? Impossible! If anyone ever tried, what would happen? His father would beat him, of course, because this request means he wants the father to die.

All three characters are now on stage: the father, the younger son and the older son. *The younger son* makes a deliberate choice to wound his father's heart and breaks relationships with all his family. He hurts the entire family by requesting one-third of the assets. He cuts himself off from his roots, from his real inheritance.

The older son knew what his brother was planning but refused to do what he ought to do: be the mediator. In a village quarrel the two never make up directly; rather negotiation through a third party must happen. The older son should have been the reconciler; he should have stepped in at once and tried to reconcile his brother to the father. But he was silent. He should have done it for the sake of his father, but he refused. This resulted in another broken relationship. Furthermore, in his culture the father could not bid his younger son good-bye. The older brother should have intervened and pleaded with his brother, "Don't leave. Your father is an old man, you may never see him again." But the older son failed to do what his culture expected of him.

The father did not refuse the younger son's request nor did he mete out punishment. No, he granted the death wish and did what no village father would ever do: he divided the property between them. *But* he refused to break relationship even though the son did.

The younger brother. A few days later, the younger son gathered all he had and travelled to a distant country. He burned his bridges behind him and left. The only thing that followed him was "the broken heart of the father." While away, he squandered his property in dissolute living. When he had spent everything, a severe famine took place throughout that country and he began to be in need. So he went and hired himself out, glued himself, clung to one of the citizens of that country, who sent him to his fields to feed the pigs—he probably didn't want him at all so he gave him the most terrible job in an attempt to get rid of him.

There he was, the rebellious, stubborn son, a Jew, one who abhorred swine. If he had any honour left, he would have refused. He would gladly have filled himself with the pods that the pigs were eating, and no one gave him anything. He ended up roaming at will in the village, eating whatever there was on the ground.

While out there in that shameful and disgusting situation, his memory clicked in and he thought of home and the relationships he had left. When he came to himself, he said, "How many of my father's hired hands have bread enough and to spare, but here I am dying of hunger! I will get up and go to my father, and I will say to him, 'Father, I have sinned against heaven and before you; I am no longer worthy to be called your son; treat me as one of your hired hands'" (v.17–19).

He had been willing to be a casual labourer abroad; now he would be ready to live in the village, not at home. All he wanted was to eat—that's all. He was not yet ready for reconciliation. So he set off and went to his father.

What should he expect? What would be considered normal practice in the village? The whole village knew the young man had left in disgrace and shame. He would return in disgrace and expect nothing more than being forced to walk or run the gauntlet of the village boys if he ever hoped to arrive at his own doorstep. He could expect nothing more than that his father would remain aloof and keep his distance. All the son could do was to sit outside the gate, waiting, finally asking if he might see his father. This would be normal. But what actually did happen? The totally unheard of, unthinkable.

The father. *"But* while he was still far off, his father saw him" (v.20). I suppose he was waiting and hoping and looking. He recognized the forlorn figure on the path, and was filled with compassion, not suspicion. He ran and flung his arms around his son, in spite of the lingering smell of pigs, and kissed him.

The father broke community solidarity; he ran, raced. This doesn't strike us as special—we know of 60–70-year-olds running 26-mile marathons. But in that culture no one over 30 ever ran; it was very undignified for an elderly man to run. Aristotle said, "Great men never run in public."

As he ran, he gathered his robe, showing his undergarments, another shameful thing. A patriarch runs for no one! And the gang of village urchins, who had formed the gauntlet for the young man to pass through, was distracted from hounding the young man, from making it difficult for him to run the gauntlet. Their attention was drawn to this strange spectacle, never before seen in the village, of a father racing strange spectacle, never before seen in the village, of a father racing down main street, shaming himself, abandoning all sense of propriety, for the sake of greeting his erring child. The son expected ruthless hostility on entering his village; instead he experienced an unexpected visual demonstration of love and humiliation. The father's acts said more than words ever could. He took upon himself the shame and humiliation belonging to the son.

Half the village had followed and the father spoke, restoring the son to himself and to the whole community. He kissed the son again and again, a sign of reconciliation and forgiveness—nothing more, nothing less. Here we have the physical demonstration of self-emptying love and suffering. The exuberance of the greeting was amazing. The son who merited scorn and shame from his townspeople, who should have been subjected to a rigorous inquiry and confession, was forgiven on the spot.

Then the son said, "Father, I have sinned against heaven and before you. I am no longer worthy to be called your son" (v. 18–19).

The young man did not offer to become a servant. He had no more suggestions for his father. He was completely overwhelmed by the father's greeting and outpouring of love. He knew he could not make up for the wounded heart of the father.

Then the father said to his slaves, "Quickly bring out a robe, the best one, and put it on him; put a ring on his finger and sandals on his feet" (v. 22).

What did this mean? "Dress him as my son, in my best robe." He would attend the banquet in the father's most elegant robe symbolizing restoration to sonship, no strings attached. The ring was a signet, a sign of authority; the shoes indicated sonship—slaves go barefoot, sons wear shoes; the robe symbolized leadership. The servants dressed him as they would a master. The son was restored in all his relationship and received a public welcome in the village.

The father continued, "And get the fatted calf and kill it, and let us eat and celebrate, for this son of mine was dead and is alive again; he was lost and is found" (v. 23–24).

The highest honour shown anyone was to slaughter a grain-fed beef for him. And they began to celebrate. All was gift of pure grace, totally undeserved and the son knew it.

The older son. One relationship was still in need: the older brother. "Now his elder son was in the field; and when he came and approached the house, he heard music and dancing. He called one of the slaves and asked what was going on. He replied, 'Your brother has come, and your father has killed the fatted calf because he has got him back safe and sound'" (v. 25–27).

"Then he became angry and refused to go in" (v. 28).

But it was the duty of older son to be head waiter symbolizing, "You, our guests, are so great that our sons are your servants." It was standard practice for oldest sons to serve choice food to all, especially to the honoured guest, who in this case was his own brother. Not to do so was an insult. He could not stay aloof. His refusal was a public and intentional insult to his father.

Word of the son's refusal reached the father and the guests. A public scene had developed, one as serious as the younger son's earlier request and departure. Again the father faced some options: agree with the older son and provide a calf for him as well; or defend himself and his actions and scold the son for his selfishness. He did neither; he did not disagree or belittle. Instead the father came out and began to plead with him.

But the elder son answered his father, accusing him of favouritism and declaring himself out of the family: "Listen! For all these years I have been working like a slave for you, and I have never disobeyed your command; yet you have never given me even a young goat so that I might celebrate with my friends. But when this son of yours came back, who has devoured your property with prostitutes, you killed the fatted calf for him!" (v. 29–30).

Then the father said to him, "Son, you are always with me, and all that is mine is yours" (v. 31).

Normally, the father was expected to be furious. Instead, we have another outpouring of love and respect: "Son . . .".

"But we had to celebrate and rejoice, because this brother of yours was dead and has come to life; he was lost and has been found" (v.32).

Two sons: one was out of touch and away; the other out of touch but at home. Both rebelled and broke the father's heart. Both ended up in a far country, one physical, the other spiritual. Yet the father showed the same unexpected love shown to both.

The gracious God. What does it feel like to be in on this drama? On one level this can be seen as a family situation, relationships between parents and children. But on another level this is what Jesus is telling his critics, about how he is with sinners and how God is with sinners, with publicans and outcasts, as well as with the Pharisees, the outstanding citizens. The younger son depicts those people who rebel openly and leave, but eventually come to their senses and come home to be embraced by God, the gracious one. The older son depicts those who tow the line outwardly, but inwardly are as lost and destitute as the others. They are the outstanding citizens who are frightfully lost at home.

Perhaps this story, more than any other in the Bible, shows us what is in your heart and in mine, and shows us clearly how amazingly gracious and welcoming God is to each of us. Where are you standing on this stage? Are you with the younger son who has come home or with the older brother who refuses to come home? You and I know where we stand. God, the heavenly father, is waiting. That's what Good Friday and Easter are about.

16

ADAM AND CHRIST, YOU AND I

*Now the serpent was more crafty than any other wild animal that
the Lord God had made. He said to the woman, "Did God say,
'You shall not eat from any tree in the garden'?" The woman
said to the serpent, "We may eat of the fruit of the trees in the
garden; but God said, 'You shall not eat of the fruit of the tree
that is in the middle of the garden, nor shall you touch it, or you
shall die.'" But the serpent said to the woman, "You will not die;
for God knows that when you eat of it your eyes will be opened,
and you will be like God, knowing good and evil." So when the
woman saw that the tree was good for food, and that it was a
delight to the eyes, and that the tree was to be desired to make
one wise, she took of its fruit and ate; and she also gave some to
her husband, who was with her, and he ate. Then the eyes of both
were opened, and they knew that they were naked; and they
sewed fig leaves together and made loincloths for themselves*
(Genesis 3:1–7).

*Then Jesus was led up by the Spirit into the wilderness to be
tempted by the devil. He fasted forty days and forty nights, and
afterwards he was famished. The tempter came and said to him,
"If you are the Son of God, command these stones to become
loaves of bread." But he answered, "It is written, 'One does not
live by bread alone, but by every word that comes from the mouth
of God.'"*

*Then the devil took him to the holy city and placed him on the
pinnacle of the temple, saying to him, "If you are the Son of God,
throw yourself down; for it is written, 'He will command his
angels concerning you,' and 'On their hands they will bear you
up, so that you will not dash your foot against a stone.'" Jesus
said to him, "Again it is written, 'Do not put the Lord your God
to the test.'"*

Again, the devil took him to a very high mountain and showed

First preached in February 1996 at First Mennonite Church, Winnipeg,
Manitoba.

him all the kingdoms of the world and their splendour; and he said to him, "All these I will give you, if you will fall down and worship me." Jesus said to him, "Away with you, Satan! for it is written, 'Worship the Lord your God, and serve only him.'" Then the devil left him, and suddenly angels came and waited on him (Matthew 4:1–11).

Robert Fulgham is the author of the book *Everything I Need to Know I Learned in Kindergarten.* In his latest book, *From Beginning to End: The Rituals of Our Lives,* he lists a number of propositions: to be human is to be religious; to be religious is to be mindful; to be mindful is to pay attention; and to pay attention is to sanctify existence. He maintains that rituals are one way in which attention is paid; rituals transform the ordinary into the holy; rituals create sacred time; and rituals may be public, private or secret.

During Lent Christians all over the world enter into sacred time, a time of public ritual. Lent is that time of the church year when we pay particular attention to the meaning of our lives in light of the life and death of Jesus Christ. This is a public ritual which will have implications for each of our lives, thus becoming private as well. Each of us will have the opportunity to deal with life in the light of Jesus' life and death.

Lent offers us a unique opportunity to reflect on some of the key issues of life, issues which affect us at the core of our being. We have read selected words from ancient texts, out of Genesis and Matthew. And on first reading we may have wondered, "What, if anything, do these ancient words have to do with me? What do these words first written in Hebrew and in Greek have to do with us?"

We might want to say, "Nothing, nothing at all; there is no connection."

We might want to say, "I hope this isn't a mirror which forces me to ask myself the awkward question, 'Am I seeing myself here?'"

We might be ready to say, "Hey, that's me; that's how I am. Even though I live centuries later, even though the old texts reach back into prehistory, in spite of all that, there is truth here. Truth about the human condition, truth about God and truth about myself and my life. Sometimes I wish this weren't a portrait of me and my neighbours—but it insists on making that claim. Maybe I should give it some attention. Of course I don't have to accept the portrait as true, but at any rate I should take a good look at it."

If we pay attention, then we notice right away that these old words are theological. They insist on connecting our lives with whatever God is up to. They remind me that long before Robert Fulgham wrote his lines, "To be human is to be religious and to be religious is to be mindful," the ancient writer had already given a religious interpretation of the human condition. We might consider our condition from a psychological or anthropological or philosophical viewpoint, but the question might haunt us, "Is the analysis adequate to deal with some of the things we deal with all the time—self, selfishness, pride, violence and sin? Do education or philosophy or science solve the problem of conflict and violence, the outer evidence that something is wrong at the core of our being? It seems they do not. Daily we are reminded of human's inhumanity to each other, of dreadful and tragic things happening in Tel Aviv, Canary Wharf, Garden City or the retired couple attacked in their home in Ashern. Is there an answer to these questions which return and haunt us at every turn? Is there an answer to the gnawing realization that at the core there is indeed a deep hunger for something dependable, something which will address the root cause of personal and social trouble which we all know about?

Consider the ancient story. It assumes that God had intentions for us as humans. God expected certain things: that we accept our creatureliness under the rule of the Creating God, that we see ourselves in our rightful place, not at the centre but under the One who is the centre. The ancient story shows that humans missed the bulls-eye, the bulls-eye of God's intention for all people, and they went astray. They gave in to their inner desire to replace God at the centre with themselves.

They said, "We refuse our God-intended position in the scheme of things. And yes, we do want to be like God. In fact we want to be in God's place."

They refused to live within the garden of freedom with the one prohibition not to eat of the fruit of that one tree. They took of the fruit and they ate—breaking fellowship with God by asserting themselves. They placed themselves at the centre; then they went into hiding, very much aware that they had done something that didn't fit the plan God had for them.

At the close of the day God is pictured as going for a stroll in the garden. God is pictured as a hunter with the questions: "Adam and Eve, where are you?"

Didn't the all-knowing Creator know where they were? I think God knew but wanted to know whether Adam and Eve were aware where they had ended up—in hiding, trying to go undetected by the Lord God.

God's question caught them up short and the blaming and accusing, passing the buck of responsibility began. Adam blamed Eve and they blamed the serpent for having asked the question which connected with a desire deep within the soul.

The result of all this was symbolized by their being booted out of the garden and prevented from coming back in. More than that, the action of these two primitives had an impact which reaches into all succeeding generations, into every person's existence, into your life and into mine. Since then all humans have been leaning on the inside, all tilting in the same direction. All of us have this deep-seated tendency in the same direction, toward self as the centre and away from God. That is the religious, biblical interpretation of the human condition.

Of course we can wish it weren't so, but our wishing changes nothing. Or we can try denying that this ancient story is true, but our denying does not change anything either—each of us has confirmed the move that Adam and Eve made and have made it our own. The Bible has a code word for this narrative description of the human condition: sin. What the story boils down to is that all humanity, each one and everyone, you and I, are in that same condition: we are sinners.

We stand before the mirror of this ancient story, and we admit, "That's us. Yes, that's me right there in this story. I am Adam or Eve."

And the seeking God is walking in the Garden of our lives asking the same old questions: "Where are you? Where are you in relation to me? Where are you in relation to others? Where are you in relation to the rest of the created order?"

Centuries later, among all the descendants of this Adam and this Eve, there stood another Adam. The apostle Paul called Christ the second Adam. Adam number two. He too was tempted—first in the desert, and later the night before his death on the cross. He too found himself wrestling in the Garden but it wasn't God asking. "Adam, where are you?" No, this time it was the second Adam asking, "God, where are you when I need you? Why have you forsaken me?"

And what happened? The second Adam whom we remember during these six weeks before Easter did not do what the first Adam did. Rather, he accepted his position in the scheme of God's plan. Paul puts it this way: ". . . though he was in the form of God (the first Adam had been in God's image too), [Jesus] did not regard equality with God as something to be exploited" (Philippians 2:6). The first Adam had fallen for the tempter's suggestion that if you eat of this tree you will be like God and exploited the temptation to become like God, the Creator. But the second Adam, Jesus, resisted the temptation to claim equality. He accepted identity with humans as the son of humanity and "emptied himself, . . . humbled himself, and became obedient to the point of death, even death on a cross" (2:8). In the first Garden there was a tree associated with disobedience and death; in the Garden of Gethsemane with the second Adam there was another tree, not one associated with disobedience and death and not the symbol of humanity's turning against God. No, this one stands for obedience leading to death, death leading to life, by resurrection.

As a full human being Jesus could have succumbed as all before him had, but he chose to live the way God intended him to live. He was obedient in the way the first Adam should have been, and the way we should have been: denying himself and accepting God's role for him. He resisted the tilt inside each of us; he gave God the rightful place at the centre. He is the second Adam—humans the way they should have turned out in the first place, but didn't. By the first Adam there was planted in each of us that leaning toward sin, self and pride; by this second Adam all humanity is offered the *remedy* for the tilt toward sin. Do we deserve this chance? No. But God throughout the Bible is God who is gracious and wanting to help, willing to sacrifice so that humans can be what they were intended to be. And in the second Adam each of us is given the opportunity to accept the undeserved gift, the correction which tilts us in the direction of God at the centre.

What are we left with? We are left with a real choice: to continue to identify with the first Adam, the one who messed up and tried to hide from God; or to claim our identity with the second Adam, the one who did things right and was glorified by God. This religious interpretation of things says as clearly as day that all are affected by the failure of the first, and that all can be made right with God by the representative action of the second Adam, the one we name Jesus Christ.

In Christ, the second Adam, God has opened the door to a new relationship with himself. Now when God the hunter asks the question, "Where are you?" we may answer, "We are with your Son, the second Adam; we do not want to stand with the first Adam; we do not want to live in hiding from you, but in fellowship with you; we do not want to accuse and blame others for the mess of our lives, but accept the ancient verdict that we are in fact sinners and need outside help to come out of hiding."

We stand with him in repentance and gratitude. We are sorry for our sins and, standing with him, we accept the obedience Jesus lived and offered as being somehow for us, that his dying and rising were not only his own but were done on behalf of all who fell with the first Adam but want to rise with the second. The consequences of our sin are atoned for, and we are set into a right relationship with God, and given the grace to live life as God intended us to live it from the beginning. When we choose to stand with the second Adam, we can also say the words of the Psalm we heard at the beginning: "Blessed are those whose transgression is forgiven, whose sin is covered" (Psalm 32:1), or as another Psalm puts it: "Bless the Lord, O my soul and do not forget all his benefits—who forgives all your sin, . . . who redeems your life" (Psalm 103:2–3).

We have no choice about the mess we got into with the first Adam, but we do have the option of claiming the second Adam as our true prototype. Let us not forget to thank God during this Lenten season. Amen.

17

UNEXPECTED JOY

Lesslie Newbigin, a Christian leader from India, tells the story of a communist leader Buckarin who, in the 1920s, travelled from Moscow to Kiev to address a large communist rally. His topic: The Folly of Believing in God. In his speech he attempted to show how utterly naive it was to believe in God. When he finally concluded, the crowd was absolutely still. Opportunity was given for questions.

An Orthodox priest asked for the floor and when he came to the podium, he greeted the crowd with the traditional Easter greeting, "Christ is risen!"

As one man the crowd stood and replied, "He is risen indeed!"

The priest returned to his seat. The communist leader made no reply. There was nothing to be said.

"Christ is risen. He is risen indeed" is heard around the world today. And the world has very little to say to these word. Ever since the first Easter, this profession has been on the lips of Jesus' followers.

But such a confession was not easy to come by. The joy that we express at Easter time was not a simple matter for the early disciples. This joy was born, it emerged out of an intense struggle of faith. It was unexpected.

C.S. Lewis has written a book, *Surprised by Joy*. I reread parts of it this week. In this book Lewis tells how he forsook the faith of early childhood and youth and pursued the paths of atheism and agnosticism. Through a series of experiences and circumstances he returned to embrace faith in God and, finally, the unexpected joy of faith in Jesus as the risen Lord. He was surprised by joy when he came to accept Jesus and commit his life to him. At the end of an intense and long struggle, he was surprised by joy.

When we read the stories of the early disciples, we notice the same: after an intense struggle they too come to joy unexpectedly. I will share the stories of three of those persons who were surprised by joy at Easter.

First preached on Easter Sunday 1982 at First Mennonite Church, Winnipeg, Manitoba.

Mary Magdalene: joy after sorrow

Mary stood weeping outside the tomb. As she wept, she bent over to look into the tomb; and she saw two angels in white, sitting where the body of Jesus had been lying, one at the head and the other at the feet. They said to her, "Woman, why are you weeping?" She said to them, "They have taken away my Lord, and I do not know where they have laid him." When she had said this, she turned around and saw Jesus standing there, but she did not know that it was Jesus. Jesus said to her, "Woman, why are you weeping? Whom are you looking for?" Supposing him to be the gardener, she said to him, "Sir, if you have carried him away, tell me where you have laid him, and I will take him away." Jesus said to her, "Mary!" She turned and said to him in Hebrew, "Rabbouni!" (which means Teacher). Jesus said to her, "Do not hold on to me, because I have not yet ascended to the Father. But go to my brothers and say to them, 'I am ascending to my Father and your Father, to my God and your God.'" Mary Magdalene went and announced to the disciples, "I have seen the Lord;" and she told them that he had said these things to her (John 20:11–18).

On the first day of the week the sorrowing Mary Magdalene returned to the tomb. Two days earlier, her friend, Jesus of Nazareth, had died. Any one of us who has lost a loved one in death knows what she felt like. It's understandable that she returned to the site of the tomb to express her grief.

As she approached the tomb, fear gripped her heart, for the tomb stood open and the body of the Lord was no longer there. Immediately she assumed that someone had desecrated his body and stolen it. In her bewilderment she ran to the disciples and shared her discovery. Then she returned to the tomb to express her grief.

Even though the Lord addressed her, "Woman, why are you crying? Who is it you are looking for?" it was impossible for her to recognize him. She thought he must be the gardener.

Why wasn't she able to recognize him? The answer is certainly related to her sorrow. Her grief, her tears prevented her from identifying him who stood near by. Grief captivated her attention. She couldn't get it out of her mind even for a moment. So great was her pain, so deep her sorrow, that she was unable to think clearly. That's the way it is with us too when we find ourselves in a valley as dark as death. We cannot see, cannot recognize the Lord either.

Another factor may well have been that she was too ready to bring an accusation, to blame whoever was near by: "They have taken the Lord from the tomb. If you took him, tell me where you have put him." So common, isn't it? When problems overwhelm us, we are quick to lay blame on others—on anyone who happens to be near by. But grief is not solved that way.

The text also suggests that Mary looked in the wrong direction: into the tomb. When Jesus finally called her by name, she turned around. Just to gaze at the tomb, to focus on the problem at hand, was not the solution. She had to turn away from the tomb and look at him. When Mary heard her name called, she was surprised by joy. Her eyes were opened, her burden lifted. Out of the ashes of despair and grief emerged the flower of hope: faith in the risen Christ.

The Lord is risen indeed! He knows your name and mine too, your sorrow and your pain. And each of us too can have the unexpected joy when we realize that the risen Christ is close at hand, present to us; that he has a deep concern for each one. He is risen indeed!

The Emmaus disciples: shattered hopes

On that same day two of them were going to a village called Emmaus, about seven miles from Jerusalem, and talking with each other about all these things that had happened. While they were talking and discussing, Jesus himself came near and went with them, but their eyes were kept from recognizing him. And he said to them, "What are you discussing with each other as you walk along?" They stood still, looking sad. Then one of them, whose name was Cleopas, answered him, "Are you the only stranger in Jerusalem who does not know the things that have taken place there in these days?" He asked them, "What things?" They replied, "The things about Jesus of Nazareth, who was a prophet mighty in deed and word before God and all the people, and how our chief priests and leaders handed him over to be condemned to death and crucified him. But we had hoped that he was the one to redeem Israel. Yes, and besides all this, it is now the third day since these things took place. Moreover, some women of our group astounded us. They were at the tomb early this morning and when they did not find his body there, they came back and told us that they had indeed seen a vision of angels who said that he was alive. Some of those who were with us went to the tomb and found it just as the women had said; but they did not see him." Then he said to them, "Oh , how foolish you are, and how slow of heart to believe all that the prophets have declared! Was it not necessary that the Messiah should suffer these things and then enter into his glory?" Then beginning with Moses and all the prophets, he interpreted to them the things about himself in all the scriptures.

As they came near the village to which they were going, he walked ahead as if he were going on. But they urged him strongly, saying, "Stay with us, for it is almost evening and the day is now nearly over." So he went in to stay with them. When he was at the table with them, he took the bread, blessed and broke it, and gave it to them. Then their eyes were opened, and they recognized him; and he vanished from their sight. They said to each other, "Were not our hearts burning within us while he was talking to us on the road, while he was opening the scriptures to us?" That same hour they got up and returned to Jerusalem; and they found the eleven and their companions gathered together. They were saying, "The Lord has risen indeed, and he has appeared to Simon!" Then they told what had happened on the road, and how he had been made known to them in the breaking of the bread (Luke 24:13–35).

As the two disciples walked along the dusty path from Jerusalem to Emmaus, they talked with each other and admitted how keenly disappointed they were: "We had hoped that he would be the one to set Israel free." Their disappointment was rooted in that fact that their expectations had been off-base. They assumed that the Messiah must come with force, crush the opposition and establish his rule. Naturally when he was crucified and laid in the tomb they were disappointed.

We too are disappointed when things don't work out for us the way we envisioned them. But these disciples stumbled across unexpected joy as well. As the stranger joined them and spoke with them, they listened and their expectations, their assumptions, were changed: "How foolish you are, how slow you are to believe everything the prophets said. Was it not necessary for the Messiah to suffer these things and then to enter his glory" (24:25–26).

The stranger opened the scriptures to them and in the evening as they stopped to eat, "their eyes were opened and they recognized him." Unexpected joy! Something they had not counted on at all. "Wasn't it like a fire burning in us when he talked to us on the road and explained the scriptures to us?" After they were willing to have their expectations revised according to God's plan, then their eyes were opened and they recognized in the stranger the presence of their risen Lord.

Perhaps we too have expectations which have disappointed us. We may have thought that our life's fate was unfair, or that our spouse ought not to have been taken by death, or it should have been better in this respect or another. "We had hoped" are words uttered by many thoughtful persons (parents) when they realize that life has not worked out the way they had it figured out. They felt that if God is almighty, he certainly could have let things work out better; if God is love, he would certainly care. When things work out differently than we had expected, then we too experience keen disappointment.

But like the two disciples, we too can be surprised by joy if we allow our expectations to be revised by hearing the Word in a fresh way. We too may have the unexpected joy of realizing that midst our deep disappointment the risen Christ is present. This unexpected joy also came after an intense struggle of faith.

Thomas, the doubter

But Thomas (who was called the Twin), one of the twelve, was not with them when Jesus came. So the other disciples told him, "We have seen the Lord." But he said to them, "Unless I see the mark of the nails in his hands, and put my finger in the mark of the nails and my hand in his side, I will not believe."

A week later, his disciples were again in the house, and Thomas was with them. Although the doors were shut, Jesus came and stood among them and said, "Peace be with you." Then he said to Thomas, "Put your finger here and see my hands. Reach out your hand and put it in my side. Do not doubt but believe." Thomas answered him, "My Lord and my God!" Jesus said to him, "Have you believed because you have seen me? Blessed are those who have not seen and yet have come to believe" (John 20:24–29).

Thomas, one of the twelve, was absent on Easter day when the Lord appeared to the disciples in the upper room. Later, when Thomas showed up, they told him, "Thomas, Jesus is risen!" Did he believe the good news? No. "Unless I see the scars of the nails in his hands and put my finger on those scars and my hand on his side, I will not believe."

Everyone who struggles with sincere doubts feels like a relative of Thomas's. And it is significant that the New Testament gives us this portrait of him. Many doubters have been helped by this story.

But not all are to be lumped in the same category. Some doubters reject all evidence as insignificant, inconsequential. They pride themselves by saying, "I will not believe, no matter what anyone says." They are closed-minded doubters.

Others are thoroughly confused. They cannot grasp things and do not move to a decision. Such doubters are unprepared to take the steps of responsible decision-making and commitment.

Still other are believing doubters—or doubting believers. The father in Mark 9:24 expressed this with the words, "I believe. Help my unbelief." Such a person has discovered the weaknesses in his own faith. Despite the continuing struggle with serious doubts and questions, he or she is still prepared to confess, "I believe." Such a person wants to believe and is prepared to risk belief.

Thomas surely is among those who were sincere doubters. In part his sincerity lay in that he was not prepared to say that he believed when, in fact, he did not. He was not sure whether he ought to believe what his friends were saying. He wanted to have surety of faith, *but* on the basis of his personal experience. He was open to consider new evidence. He remained with the disciples for he was a searcher for truth. He doubted in order to be certain.

Many of us have similar experiences. That should not disturb us. Sincere doubting, like Thomas's, is to be welcomed because it leads to new experiences and deeper faith.

The Lord appeared to the disciples again, greeting them with the words, "Peace be with you!" When Thomas saw him, Jesus invited him to examine the nail prints and place his hand on his side. Unexpected joy! Then Thomas too could confess, "My Lord and my God."

This doubter experienced a joyful turning. He confessed openly and freely that he was now convinced: "He is risen indeed!" This confession did not come easily. It was the result of a struggle of faith. Even today those words are only uttered after someone who wants to believe has named the doubts, then is able to move to the unexpected joy of the confession, "He is risen indeed!"

I challenge each of you on this Easter day to ponder anew the confession of the early church, that Jesus is risen indeed. And to be open to the unexpected joy that comes in this commitment to him. All those who are surprised by joy are eager to live for him.

May the Lord strengthen our faith and our commitment. May we live in fellowship with him who is present with us. And may each of us and we as a congregation stand firm and steady, abounding in the work of the Lord, knowing that in him it is not in vain.

18

FREE—TO CHOOSE A MASTER

Now the serpent was more crafty than any other wild animal that the Lord God had made. He said to the woman, "Did God say, 'You shall not eat from any tree in the garden'?" The woman said to the serpent, "We may eat of the fruit of the trees in the garden; but God said, 'You shall not eat of the fruit of the tree that is in the middle of the garden, nor shall you touch it, or you shall die.'" But the serpent said to the woman, "You will not die; for God knows that when you eat of it your eyes will be opened, and you will be like God, knowing good and evil." So when the woman saw that the tree was good for food, and that it was a delight to the eyes, and that the tree was to be desired to make one wise, she took of its fruit and ate; and she also gave some to her husband, who was with her, and he ate. Then the eyes of both were opened, and they knew that they were naked; and they sewed fig leaves together and made loincloths for themselves (Genesis 3:1–7).

So Ahab sent to all the Israelites, and assembled the prophets at Mount Carmel. Elijah then came near to all the people, and said, "How long will you go limping with two different opinions? If the Lord is God, follow him; but if Baal, then follow him." The people did not answer him a word (1 Kings 18:20–21).

Do you not know that if you present yourselves to anyone as obedient slaves, you are slaves of the one whom you obey, either of sin, which leads to death, or of obedience, which leads to righteousness? But thanks be to God that you, who were once slaves of sin, have become obedient from the heart to the form of teaching to which you were entrusted, and that you, having been set free from sin, have become slaves of righteousness. I am speaking in human terms, because of your natural limitations. For just as you once presented your members as slaves to impurity and to greater and greater iniquity, so now present your

---

First preached in January 1970 at First Mennonite Church, Winnipeg, Manitoba.

members as slaves to righteousness for sanctification.

When you were slaves of sin, you were free in regard to righteousness. So what advantage did you then get from the things of which you now are ashamed? The end of those things is death. But now that you have been freed from sin and enslaved to God, the advantage you get is sanctification. The end is eternal life. For the wages of sin is death, but the free gift of God is eternal life in Christ Jesus our Lord (Romans 6:16–23).

"Who cares about society and its traditions. I'm free to live the kind of life that I choose to live. If I want to live an illicit sex life or smoke pot or take a trip or two, that's my personal decision. I'm free." These are the words of a young man speaking on "Cross-Country Check-up" (CBC Radio, November 23, 1969). These words thrust the current quest for freedom before us for our attention.

Everyone wants to be free. Our time stresses freedom and encourages its expression. On a personal level the drive to freedom comes to expression in statements like the following: "I'm sick and tired of school. I'm quitting. I want to be free." Or, "I'm free. I can do as I please. What I do with my life is no one else's business."

A maturing teenager rebels against authority with some of his rebellion being taken out on his parents: "Why does my life have to be hemmed in by your restrictions, your beliefs, your traditions? I want out. I want to be free." On a social level much of the drive for freedom has been focused on the civil rights movement in the United States or on Vietnam War protest activities or on the hippie-style reaction against the values and ways of the predominant culture.

All of this ferment for freedom finds its echoes in our own feelings and thoughts. We recognize that sometimes we too have the same kinds of urges. And this ferment begins to raise serious questions in our minds about the nature of freedom for human beings. Do you want to be free in 1970? That will depend on your definition of freedom. Do you want to be free of all restraints: "I want to do as I please"? Do you want to resolve inner conflicts as you go through life? Does freedom mean only freedom to rebel?

Let me say that there is no such thing as being without restraints; there is no such thing as being absolutely free. Yet Jesus claimed, "If the Son makes you free, you will be free indeed" (John 8:36). What does "free indeed" mean? My basic point is that we are free only when we are in bondage. We are free only to the extent that we have a choice over who (or what) our master will be.

Bishop Gerald Kennedy of Los Angeles uses the illustration of a man adrift in his boat at sea. He is free—but lost. Or think of a man who roams in a jungle. He can go anywhere he pleases but he is lost in that jungle and quite impotent. The man adrift at sea finds freedom when he has "a star to steer by;" the man in the jungle finds his freedom when he establishes radio contact with the ranger station. Then he is free to do constructive exploration.

Again, think of a train. If a train could think, "I want to be free of these tracks. They are so bothersome and restrictive. Always I have to go the same route. I'll break free of these track; I'll go where I want to go." And he does. He lunges off the tracks, free, but thoroughly stuck in the dirt. The train's freedom to arrive at its destiny is determined by its bondage to the tracks. They seem restrictive; actually they are liberating.

Let us turn to the marriage relationship. Is marriage freedom or bondage? It is both. Once a couple has come through the cross-fire of conflicting loyalties, they bind themselves to each other (freely), yet they find true freedom. They may now be free with each other and for each other. Their relationship may grow and they are free from the claims of all other suitors. Bound to one and free from all others.

When we consider freedom in this light, we link it to our search for identity. We are not only asked *who* we are but also *whose* we are. To whom are you bound?

Christians are persons who have found that freedom comes by way of a binding commitment. This theme appears again and again in the scriptures. "Choose this day whom you will serve" (Joshua 24:15). In the paragraphs preceding this challenge, we find a review of all that God had already done for his people. The choice is not to be made in a vacuum but in the context of God's prior, gracious acts. It is impossible for the biblical writers to conceive of persons who have no god at all. So when God speaks he asks for total allegiance and the total rejection of every competing sovereignty (Paul Minear, *Eyes of Faith,* 72).

In the book of Genesis we find further evidence of this theme in the story of the Garden and the choice to be made. Adam and Eve are placed in the garden, free to have dominion under God but with one restrictive fence: "Of one tree you shall not eat." We know the story. We were there—in our own "Garden." We wanted total freedom: "Down with that fence." And down it went. Did it break God? No, but it did break freedom; it hurled man [and woman] into a bondage which was not at all creative any more. They lost their freedom to live in fellowship and harmony—within bounds.

James Smart writes,

> Man, in so far as he is his own master, is incapable of freedom. He longs to be free and yet is incapable of freedom. He longs to be free but plunges himself into one slavery after another. The Christian Gospel says that man cannot be free within himself except under the mastery of God (Smart, *Recovery of Humanity*, 73).
>
> ... freedom becomes ours at the moment when the living God enters our lives and we surrender forever the right to do what we like. . . . If God is his master, then no power in heaven or in earth can ever enslave him. Slavery: work, possessions, pleasure, worry, anger, lust. "Freedom" by many who believe only in their own right to do what they like (Smart: 75).

Another illustrative incident comes from the ministry of Elijah (1 Kings 18: 17–39). The Israelites had been led into thinking that they could "double-date" God and Baal. The issue came to a focus on the slopes of Mount Carmel and was spoken by Elijah: "How long will you go limping with two different opinions? If the Lord is God, follow him; but if Baal, then follow him" (v. 21). In other words, Elijah says, "You must make up your mind whose you will ultimately be and whom you will serve with your whole heart. You must make a commitment which is a free choice—with both a binding and freeing effect."

As we consider Jesus' ministry, the same theme comes through loud and clear: "No one can serve two masters; for either he will hate the one and love the other, or he will be devoted to the one and despise the other" (Matthew 6:24). When Jesus called people to join him, he put the issues squarely before them "Calling me Lord and following me demands your highest allegiance" ("Sei ganz sein oder lass es ganz sein"—Be his alone or leave him alone completely).

Saul of Tarsus also illustrates the issue for us. As a Pharisee he was bound in one way, free in one way; but when he experienced Jesus, the Risen Lord in his life, he switched masters. He was now free from all former masters, from all contemporary competition for his loyalty, and bound to Jesus only.

The evidence is adequate: The Christian gospel tells the Good News of God's gracious act in Christ, then places before us a decision. We are free to decide who our Master or Lord will be, and as we decide we rule out other "suitors." Tomorrow does not belong to the majority; tomorrow belongs to the disciplined, the committed. As we do in marriage, let us say one basic "Yes" and that will determine a whole list of things; it binds and it liberates.

This is the basic question to be decided as we enter 1970. Many of us may think, "Well, I've made that decision some time ago." Fine. Those who are married once promised to be faithful, but that is not the end of the matter. Which marriage relationship would last without reaffirmation? For those who have made their life's commitment to Jesus earlier, this is an invitation to reaffirm that intention, to confirm that decision. For those who cannot remember making such a commitment to Jesus, this is an invitation to acknowledge him as Saviour and Lord and to promise to live under his direction.

Are you tired of "limping along" in your life? Limping along is usually the result of not consciously being sure whose we are. Let us make the decision afresh to acknowledge Jesus as our Lord, then launch ahead into 1970.

19

LET'S TALK MONEY

Take care that you do not forget the Lord your God, by failing to keep his commandments, his ordinances, and his statutes, which I am commanding you today. When you have eaten your fill and have built fine houses and live in them, and when your herds and flocks have multiplied, and your silver and gold is multiplied, and all that you have is multiplied, then do not exalt yourself, forgetting the Lord your God, who brought you out of the land of Egypt, out of the house of slavery, who led you through the great and terrible wilderness, an arid wasteland with poisonous snakes and scorpions. He made water flow for you from flint rock, and fed you in the wilderness with manna that your ancestors did not know, to humble you and to test you, and in the end to do you good. Do not say to yourself, "My power and the might of my own hand have gotten me this wealth." But remember the Lord your God, for it is he who gives you power to get wealth, so that he may confirm his covenant that he swore to your ancestors, as he is doing today. If you do forget the Lord your God and follow other gods to serve and worship them, I solemnly warn you today that you shall surely perish. Like the nations that the Lord is destroying before you, so shall you perish, because you would not obey the voice of the Lord your God (Deuteronomy 8:11–20).*

Do not store up for yourselves treasures on earth, where moth and rust consume and where thieves break in and steal; but store up for yourselves treasures in heaven, where neither moth nor rust consumes and where thieves do not break in and steal. For where your treasure is, there your heart will be also. . . . No one can serve two masters; for a slave will either hate the one and love the other, or be devoted to the one and despise the other. You cannot serve God and wealth (Matthew 6:19–21, 24).

First preached in October 1993 at First Mennonite Church, Winnipeg, Manitoba.

You will have noticed the title of my sermon. I will begin by saying what I am *not* going to talk about. I will *not* talk about our church budget, although our finance committee might like me to; I will *not* talk about how much we ought to give, although I could make some suggestions along that line; I will *not* talk about what we ought to give to, although I could provide some guidelines. I *am* going to talk about basic attitudes, choices and the options we have.

The celebration of Thanksgiving and the words of the ancient text from Deuteronomy remind us again that life presents us with options: to remember or to forget. If we choose to remember what the text says, certain things follow; if we choose to forget and ignore, then other equally certain things follow. If we choose to remember we take a particular attitude to life, to possessions and to God; if we choose to forget, we have a different set of attitudes toward life, to possessions and to God.

We do have choices to make. We are not captives in these matters. We can choose to be conformed to a selfish, worldly, materialistic view of life *or* be transformed to a new way of thinking about life, about possessions and God. Hear what the text says, "You must never think that you made yourselves wealthy by your own power and strength. Remember that it is the Lord your God who gives you the power to become rich."

Although many of us might want to excuse ourselves from the label "wealthy," we need to realize that on a world scale we are among those who are the richest. Maybe many of the Israelites did not think they were wealthy either, but in comparison to having been refugees and desert wanderers for 40 years, they were now wealthy. Of course they did not know what life would be like in the 1990s. They did not know that what was rich centuries ago in an agrarian society was nothing in comparison to our definitions and experiences with wealth today. In spite of the differences, these ancient words challenge us today to consider some important questions about money.

Each of us is creating biography, if not with words, then by the way we live. Some day, someone—or we ourselves—will pause to reflect on our lives and tell our stories. They will highlight relationships, work, interests. One category in such a story is often overlooked: it's been called a money biography. Have you ever seen one? Have you written one? I've seen one; it was very interesting and revealing. Can you imagine what a biographer could dig up on each of us if he or she were commissioned to write the story of our lives on the theme of money? There would be a report on how much we actually earned, an analysis of how we actually spent our money and, if possible, it would report our private thoughts about all this. How would you feel if such a biography were being written about you? Would you want that story to be sealed from others for a quarter century before you die? Whether we've begun writing or not, we are all in the process of creating our own money biography.

I want to talk about three options that we have about this area of life.

Option 1. We can reflect on money or treat it as a taboo subject. We can ponder the meaning of money and its power or treat it as something we simply refuse to discuss. I considered the latter option and have made a choice: I've thought about it and have chosen to talk about it.

Let's consider some random saying about money, things we hear or think from time to time

– Money is very private; it's no one else's business. In a recent survey it was shown that 95 percent of church members do not discuss finances with others in the church.

– Money talks—someone has added, "with a divided voice."

– Money makes the world go 'round.

– I'm not really that well off.

– It takes all I can do just to make ends meet.

– I worked hard for this and I deserve it.

– Enough is just a bit more than I currently have.

– Do you ever worry about money? No, just the lack of it.

– Money is one thing which morals and values completely separate.

– I shop, therefore I am ("I think, therefore I am"—Descartes).

We could probably add more proverbs to this list. All get at the basic attitudes we encounter when it comes to money.

Christian Century did a survey among church members regarding money. The following was reported in an article, "Pious Materialism: How Americans View Faith and Money" (*Christian Century*, March 3, 1993): 80 percent agreed that society is too materialistic; our wants are spiralling out of control; we admire the people who make a lot of money by working hard; 22 percent said that God doesn't care how I use my money; the church does a better job of comforting the afflicted than afflicting the comfortable; 75 percent said the church should encourage members to be less materialistic. The article argues that money is too important an issue to leave only to economists, that the power of the material over us is captivating, and that many of us are prisoners of consumerism.

If we go back further than this recent survey, back to the early church, we note that three basic attitudes prevailed. First, money is a spiritual obstacle: "If you want to enter the kingdom, sell what you have and give to the poor." Secondly, money is spiritually irrelevant. It's really beside the point. We want to work on the spiritual side of things. Everyone is on their own in this matter. Finally, money is a spiritual instrument. Paul spoke affirmatively about giving: "God loves a cheerful giver."

Several more recent quotations are positive statements about money:

"Did you know that your money is your talent and energy in portable form? It goes where you can't go; it speaks languages you can't speak; it keeps working after you go to bed. A very positive attitude, isn't it?"—Harry Emerson Fosdick

"We forget that the hallmark of biblical spirituality is its materiality, its celebration of this world's goodness."—Thomas Troeger

Note also the warnings in the Bible that riches are dangerous: "The love of money is the root of all evil." "Beware of all covetousness." And from a current writer: "Affluence is the perfect anaesthesia for helping us to forget the pain of others. It anaesthetizes conscience, compassion and concern."—David Augsburger.

Option 2. We can live with conspicuous discontent or live with conspicuous contentment. I will show what I mean by referring to two stories. Remember the story of Ahab and Naboth? Think of Ahab's money biography. He had enough of everything, more than enough, and yet he was compulsively going after more, no matter what the cost. Anyone or anything in his way would be shoved aside: "I want your vineyard and I'll get it." When he couldn't have his way, he refused to eat, lay down on his bed and turned to the wall, sulking. Ahab lived with perpetual discontent. He was trapped in the cage of his own desiring, his covetousness and greed.

Contrast that with Paul who, while sitting in a Roman prison, wrote, "I have learned to be content with whatever I have" (Philippians 4:11b). That's hard to imagine. Paul lived a life marked by conspicuous contentment. " I know what it is to have little, and I know what it is to have plenty. In any and all circumstances I have learned the secret of being well-fed and of going hungry, of having plenty and of being in need. I can do all things through him who strengthens me" (4:12–13).

We have the choice: to stand with Ahab or with Paul.

Option 3. We can live for ourselves or be generous. We can live lives wrapped up in self and with possessions, or we can strip wealth of its power over us, wrap it with grace and live for others. Again, I would like to refer to two stories to illustrate my point.

The first comes from the life of the early church in the book of Acts.

For a short time they practised community of goods, sharing everything with the others. This situation sounds ideal, yet even this noble experiment was open to abuse. One of the members, Barnabas, had a piece of real estate on an island. When there was a need, he sold it and brought the cash to the apostles for use in the community. Probably his generosity was shared in their meetings and he was duly thanked. Others all noticed—major donors get recognition.

Among those who took note was a couple. On the way home they chat about things and Ananias says to Sapphira, his wife: "You know, dear, it would be nice for us to be in the spotlight too, wouldn't it?" They agreed to sell their property. Then greed set in, "Let's give a portion of our take as though it were the whole. We'll get the recognition and, if things don't work out in the future, we'll have a nice sum put away—like our own rainy day fund."

They did it and brought their donation to the apostles. But Peter, led by the Holy Spirit, smelled a rat, deception, greed and falsehood. He confronted him and Ananias dropped dead later. Then Sapphira came to be in the spotlight with her husband. She was asked about the donation, whether this was the whole amount of the sale. "Of course," she said. Peter called her on it and she dropped dead.

Barnabas was unselfishly generous; Ananias and Sapphira were selfishly generous. Barnabas had stripped wealth of its power over him; Ananias and Sapphira were prisoners of their greed for money and recognition.

I conclude with several verses from Paul to Timothy:

> As for those who in the present age are rich, command them not to be haughty, or to set their hopes on the uncertainty of riches, but rather on God who richly provides us with everything for our enjoyment. They are to do good, to be rich in good works, generous, and ready to share, thus storing up for themselves the treasure of a good foundation for the future, so that they may take hold of the life that really is life (1 Timothy 6:17–19).

Isn't that what we are all after: life that really is life? Let us consider our options. Let us reflect on our options regarding money. Let us be thankful for all the good that we have and enjoy. Let us take some concrete steps in the direction of conspicuous contentment. Let us use our money for the good of others and to the glory of God.

20

A SACRED MOMENT, A SPECIAL COMMITMENT

If I speak in the tongues of mortals and of angels, but do not have love, I am a noisy gong or a clanging cymbal. And if I have prophetic powers, and understand all mysteries and all knowledge, and if I have all faith, so as to remove mountains, but do not have love, I am nothing. If I give away all my possessions, and if I hand over my body so that I may boast, but do not have love, I gain nothing.

Love is patient; love is kind; love is not envious or boastful or arrogant or rude. It does not insist on its own way; it is not irritable or resentful; it does not rejoice in wrongdoing, but rejoices in the truth. It bears all things, believes all things, hopes all things, endures all things.

Love never ends. But as for prophecies, they will come to an end; as for tongues, they will cease; as for knowledge, it will come to an end. For we know only in part; but when the complete comes, the partial will come to an end. When I was a child, I spoke like a child, I thought like a child, I reasoned like a child; when I became an adult, I put an end to childish ways. For now we see in a mirror dimly, but then we will see face to face. Now I know only in part; then I will know fully, even as I have been fully known. And now faith, hope, and love abide, these three; and the greatest of these is love (1 Corinthians 13).

In this hour time stops and everything focuses on you, the couple. This is a time between the times, after the before, and before the after. This moment exists for the sake of what we do here. The step that you are taking in this moment of stopped time is a very important one. It grows out of all that has happened before to you as a couple, and even to you as individuals, growing persons, prior to the beginning of your special relationship.

Today you stop—everything stops—as you mark the embarking of a journey, a journey that will take you to the end of your lives together,

---

Preached on July 18, 1992, at the wedding of John and Anne Neufeld's daughter and son-in-law, Brenda Neufeld and Robert Pankratz.

a journey in which you will be expected to be faithful to each other amidst changes: changes in each of you as you go through the adult life cycle, and changes in your life's circumstances.

This moment then is special, momentous, sacred, because you are making a covenant with each other, a covenant which will shape your existence, colour everything you do for the rest of your lives. Your covenant is expressed in the words of your vows which you have selected, words which say how you will be with and for each other for life.

Such a moment can be described as sacred. We are very much aware of each other, you of each other, you of your parents, and they of you; you aware of all the loved ones and friends who are here to celebrate with you, and they aware of you.

What can be done with such a special moment? One of the things that is done, quite unconsciously, is to remember. Memories are very much at the centre of moments such as these. For all of us who are married, this hour brings back memories of our own weddings. For your parents, there are memories of your births, your growing up years, hopes and joys, frustrations and satisfactions, and your becoming independent. And for you, memories crowd in as well: your first awareness of each other, your first encounter, getting to know each other, your growth in love and commitment, and finally your decision to marry.

Another thing, in addition to remembering, is that we can reflect on the meanings of marriage. What does it mean to make solemn vows to each other here in the presence of God and your families and friends? All of us who have come realize that today we will think about marriage: What might marriage be? What is it for us already? What might it be for you?

I'd like to say a few things about that and connect my comments with the passage in our reading from the Apostle Paul. Let's think about marriage using the image of a journey. To come to the decision to embark on a journey through life with one other person, requires an enormous amount of courage.

An American writer, Joseph Sittler, has said, "The heart of marriage is a promise. On the face of it it's a crazy promise. Two people, who have only a partial understanding of one another, stand up and make this bizarre statement that they're going to cherish and care for one another for a lifetime. . . . Marriage is a mutual acceptance of a crazy challenge to fulfil the seemingly impossible. A commitment like that takes guts."

And here you are, ready to publicly make this courageous promise to each other in our hearing. To do so says that marriage is not only feelings of love, romance and affection, but a life-long task undertaken together to journey together, to build your lives as caring, committed partners. Someone has suggested that marriage is like making a garden out of a wilderness plot: it takes clearing and tilling and seeding and weeding. And then waiting and hoping, and eventually realizing the harvest of vegetables and the beauty of a variety of flowers in what was once a patch of untilled grass. No one can approach an untilled plot of land and expect to have an instant garden. Nor do we arrive at a mature marriage instantly. It will take time and effort, listening and speaking, apologizing and forgiving, arguing and making up, and recommitting yourselves to this life-long task, again and again.

The writing of Paul points in the same direction. He speaks of a kind of love which has the power to build for life. This love is one that emerges in actions and results in building something that outlasts emotional highs and lows. For Paul, love is more than good feelings. It is a decision to act in loving ways no matter how one feels. It is the decision to build a relationship in faithful and caring, sometimes stubborn, ways. This kind of love says: "I will do the caring deed, the deed that contributes to building and not demolition."

Listen to Paul's phrases again: "Slow to lose patience, not possessive, not touchy, looking for ways of being constructive." Herein lies a blueprint for life-long building, life-long travelling together. Remind yourselves of these words often and incorporate them into your daily lives.

Marriage then, is journeying and building and, thirdly, being friends. Being married is having a special friendship with one other as with no others. Friendship, true friendship, involves taking risks. Intimate friendship means mutual exploration of the complexity that is another human being. It takes courage to give of ourselves, to be vulnerable, to share of our deepest being.

Andrew Greeley has written, "Friendship is alternation between hiding and revelation, between keeping secrets and telling them, between mystery and blatancy." Married friends love each other in a deeply committed way and, in the process, we discover our mates to be "more gifted than we had dreamed and more flawed than we had hoped" (Whitehead).

Again Paul's writing on love is amazing: "Love knows no limit to its endurance, no end to its trust, no fading of its hope. It can outlast anything. It is the one thing that still stands when all else has fallen."

Being friends with each other in marriage is no "piece of cake." It's daily, demanding, draining and rewarding. May you continue to grow in friendship in such a way that each of you "grows in the freedom of personhood and that you grow together in an incomparable unity."

I've already said that marriage is a special kind of friendship. It is being involved with one other one in mutual committed love, in sexual exclusivity and permanence. Marriage is sexually bonded friendship. Sexuality is at the core of marriage. It is the unique expression of a unique relationship and, biblically understood, is to be the celebration of all that the relationship means to you.

We have said this is a sacred moment, marking a special commitment to being partners in life, on a journey, involved in the building of a relationship, a special friendship. You will need commitment, courage and the kind of love that is spoken of by Paul in your text.

21

THE STORMS OF LIFE

Everyone then who hears these words of mine and acts on them will be like a wise man who built his house on rock. The rain fell, the floods came, and the winds blew and beat on that house, but it did not fall, because it had been founded on rock. And every one who hears these words of mine and does not act on them will be like a foolish man who built his house on sand. The rain fell, and the floods came, and the winds blew and beat against that house, and it fell—and great was its fall (Matthew 7:24–27).

I have fought the good fight, I have finished the race, I have kept the faith. From now on there is reserved for me the crown of righteousness, which the Lord, the righteous judge, will give me on that day, and not only to me but also to all who have longed for his appearing (2 Timothy 4:7–8).

The words of Jesus in Matthew 7 are often used to point out the necessity of a solid foundation in one's life: to build on Jesus' teaching. Another important thing said in these verses is that whether we build on sand or rock, the storms will come. This says that having Christ as the foundation of our lives is no assurance that we will be spared difficulties in life. The rain, winds and storm beat upon both persons' lives, whether or not they had Jesus as their foundation.

Your mother had accepted Christ into her life a long time ago and since then she sought to express that faith in her life. But she also experienced a lot of testing, particularly when your father died over 20 years ago and, more recently, with her illness. She enjoyed good health for many years as the children were growing up, but some months ago the storms began to rage in her life. Her energy waned, her illness was diagnosed, she underwent treatment, she had to give up work, she had to struggle within herself about her new situation.

No doubt many of us, as we became aware of her illness, have tried to imagine what it would be like to go through what she had to endure. One of the things we could identify with was her feeling that it simply

Preached on March 22, 1980, at the funeral of Katy D. Wiebe held at First Mennonite Church, Winnipeg, Manitoba.

wasn't fair. "Just imagine, after I was widowed, I worked and raised the children. Now that they have reached adulthood I thought I would be able to enjoy life with a little less pressure. And then, what do I get? Leukemia! It just doesn't seem fair!" I am sure that each of us in a similar situation would have the same thoughts. "And the winds blew and beat upon that house, but it did not fall, because it had been founded on the rock."

Another thing she found difficult during this storm was having the feeling of being useless. She was used to being able to work, to be responsible, to help others, to carry a fair share of the load. Now as her physical strength decreased she had to be helped. She had to accept her new position. It was hard. I know the children did not think that she was useless, but she felt it within herself. Yet even this was thought about in the light of her faith: "There must be some purpose to all of this, but I don't understand it now." "And the winds beat upon that house but it did not fall for it was built upon the rock."

Through the storms of life, through the suffering, "living hope" shines through. The writer of 1 Peter says this so clearly. He praises "the God and Father of our Lord Jesus Christ" for having given all believers a "living hope through the resurrection of Jesus Christ from the dead." He praises God for "an inheritance which is imperishable and unfading" (1 Peter 1:3–4). This writer also says that the storms that test one's life reveal "the genuineness of our faith" so that in spite of setbacks and suffering, there is a deep sense of gratitude to God. "As the outcome of your faith you obtain the salvation of your souls" (1:9).

A related image in Hebrew is the anchor that holds our lives steady no matter how much we are driven by the wind. That anchor is our hope, based on what God has done for us. This was the basis of your loved one's faith and hope during her struggle. Here she found the inner strength to bear the burden and the heat of the day. For her faith and her courage in the face of adversity we must be deeply grateful.

From the other side, this experience also has been a storm for you as a family: her illness and then this week the unexpected news of her death. It was hard to believe, yet it is true and somehow you have to come to terms with it. That is the storm in which you are now caught up. Even in the face of this death, this loss in your lives, you must go on with life. But how does one go on?

Going on means living with unanswered and unanswerable questions: why suffering? why an early death? There is a mystery side of life. We simply do not have all the answers, but we continue to hold to him who himself is the Answer.

Going on means working through the stages of grief: shock and disbelief, remembering, emotional release, emptiness and reaffirming the meaning of life.

Going on means remembering and cherishing a shared past: being grateful for all that she was to each of you, for her strength and dedication in raising the family, for many things stored away in your hearts. Going on means checking our own life's foundation. Is our life's house resting squarely on Jesus who is the only enduring foundation? Going on means knowing that the Lord who was with her is also willing to be with you.

Going on means being challenged once more by her concern for you. Paul's farewell words are appropriate: "The time of my departure has come. I have fought the good fight, I have finished the race, I have kept the faith. Henceforth there is laid up for me the crown of righteousness, . . . and not only to me but also to all who have loved his appearing" (2 Timothy 6b–8).

She says to all of us: "I have fought the good fight of faith and of life; I have tried to live by faith, to express it. Will you do the same?

"I have finished the race. It was shorter than I would have liked it to be, but I see the finish line. Will you, my friends, run your race, whether it be long or short, till you too see the finish line?

"I have kept the faith—and the Lord has kept me through all the vicissitudes of life, even through the storm of cancer. Will you, my friends, keep the faith too, no matter what comes your way?

"Now at the end I strive forward in hope for that which the Lord has in store for me: the crown of life. Will you live in this hope too? I hope you will."

Our prayer is that you as a family and all of us will remember her with gratitude and will be comforted. May you continue to experience the support of friends and loved ones and, above all, the presence of him who is life's everlasting foundation, Jesus Christ.

Sexuality,
Marriage
and
Family

22

MALE AND FEMALE HE CREATED THEM

Part I
. . . male and female he created them (Genesis 1:27b).

As part of our emphasis this month on family life, I want to preach on the subject of human sexuality. In the first sermon I will present the biblical view on sex and sexuality. In the second I will describe the distortion and contradiction of the biblical view in history, describe the sexual revolution of our time, and suggest a few directions for our time.

Some of this material is detailed and may come across more like a lecture than a sermon. But I hope a congregation of keen and alert minds will not mind thinking along with me. The background material is necessary simply so we have something to help us think clearly about issues we face in our daily living. Much of the material is derived from two books: David R. Mace, *The Christian Response to the Sexual Revolution;* and Pieter de Jong, *The Biblical View of Man.*

For some of you it may come as no surprise that "the church is the last place where you would expect plain talk about human sexuality." We are being bombarded with views and attitudes on all sides and it is legitimate to review what the Bible and the church have to say on the subject. Some persons have a negative view on sex and assume that this anti-sexual bias is rooted in the Bible. This is the first area about which we will be forced to change our minds.

Preliminary considerations At the outset let me make several points:

1) The biblical attitude shifts considerably from the early period to the New Testament. For example, polygamy was accepted in the early period, but by New Testament times monogamy was considered normal. Also, the custom of the levirate, a practice which dictated that a man had to have intercourse with his dead brother's wife, seems to have died out by New Testament times.

Two-part series preached in 1972 at First Mennonite Church, Winnipeg, Manitoba.

2) The purpose of the Bible is not to lay it on the line for every specific case. Scripture proclaims broad, basic truths and attitudes; the details are worked out by people who are caught in the midstream of life's activity. Jesus laid down two basic laws which, he said, include everything: love God, love your neighbour. This meant that the details ought to be derived from devotion to God and an understanding of people and their needs.

3) Some of Paul's comments on sex and marriage need to be read with an awareness that he believed "the time is short," life on earth will not continue for long (1 Corinthians 7:31b); therefore, why bother about marriage and sex?

4) A number of problems facing us today are simply not referred to at all in the Bible: masturbation, petting, contraception, abortion, trial marriages, sterilization, artificial insemination, genetic controls. But this does not mean that the church must not be prepared to examine these new issues with all the insight and faithfulness we can muster.

"Male and female he created them." Near the beginning of Genesis we receive the impression that God heartily approves of sex. God deliberately, intentionally, made man a sexual being. And when he was done he wasn't plagued by doubts about what he had done. God considered his handiwork and congratulated himself that it was a very noble effort: "very good." This is the first and fundamental fact about sex in the biblical view.

When the Bible speaks to sex, its writers are not tongue-tied as many persons are today. We read stories of sexual behaviour which would be considered quite unsuitable for public reading. They present us with straightforward down-to-earth accounts of how real people with sexual needs and drives acted. Sex is openly treated as part of human life.

Sex in Hebrew thought. Sex played a central role in religious thought because it was the means by which a man became a father. It was a man's religious duty to beget sons and daughters, for the Messiah would one day come from the seed of Abraham. For the Jew, begetting children was man's primary response to God. Sex was the means by which man continued the work of creation on behalf of God—pro-creation.

Family life was held in high esteem. All men were expected to marry and have children. Bridegrooms were exempted from military duty until they had time to settle the supreme business of life. It was the greatest of tragedies not to have the line continue through the male.

For us, circumcision is performed for hygienic reasons, but then it served as the mark of identity as a member of God's people—and this mark was carried on the sex organ which was considered sacred and not disreputable. In fact, the foreskin was viewed as an offering to God, a symbol that the man's whole body, his whole person was dedicated to God. With this organ he became a co-worker with God in a special sense.

In that day they had no understanding of sperm and ovum, but considered the male seed to be the future child. This seed needed to be planted in a woman's body, the womb serving only as soil or as an incubator. A wife who was unable to conceive was in real trouble, not so much for herself but especially for her husband who would be unable to fulfil his supreme religious role of becoming a father. Against this frustration, polygamy was permitted and tolerated in order to deliver a man from his predicament (for example, Hagar and Sarah).

The view that the woman contributed nothing of her essential self to the child she bore led to a curious double standard. A Hebrew husband could not be unfaithful to his wife—he was free to plant his seed wherever he willed. Hence an adulterer sinned not against his own wife but against the other woman's husband; that is, he adulterated the line. A wife was bound to bear her husband's children and so assure him of immortality. There was to be no doubt that all children born to his wife were his own. The concern was that the family line was not to be falsified. An unfaithful wife was of no use to her husband. All this means that a Hebrew man had very few choices for extra-marital affairs—only with harlots or with slave girls caught in war. A wife's prestige was determined by her ability to bear children.

In summary, for the Hebrews sex was a good gift of God to be used and enjoyed as God directed. The primary purpose of sexual union was procreation. There was no trace of sexual asceticism. The misuse of sex (adultery) was strongly condemned, but sex was not inherently evil. Like every other area of human life, it could be abused and become an occasion for sin.

Sex in the New Testament. There is much less sexual material in the New Testament. This is because the writers assumed knowledge of the Old Testament. Jesus seems to have accepted the basic goodness of sex. From his teachings we can glean the following:

1) Jesus reaffirmed the sanctity and permanence of marriage.

2) He challenged the Hebrew idea of marriage as universal duty. However, nothing he said justifies the church's later stand on celibacy.

3) He stressed that the root of all sin was inward—in attitudes, wayward impulses and the desires of the heart.

4) His attitude toward sexual sins was understanding and compas-

sion. This was in sharp contrast to the punitive attitudes of the religious leaders of the time. Jesus tried to correct the Pharisee's view that singles out sexual transgressions for violent attack.

Paul also accepted the Jewish position. He recognized the need for husbands and wives to enjoy a healthy sex life (1 Corinthians 7:2–5). Paul had a very high view of marriage, using it as an appropriate analogy of the relationship between Christ and the church.

We must acknowledge then that the Bible's view of sex is positive. Being male or female is very good and ought to serve to increase human fulfilment. In the next sermon we will consider how this high view of sexuality was distorted.

Part II

In Part I we looked at the biblical view of sexuality. In review:

1) Sexuality is one of God's good gifts. Every person is either a male human being or a female human being.

2) In marriage, sex has a two-fold purpose: procreation and mutual pleasure.

3) The Bible does not teach that we ought to be asexual, but since we can't swing that, we are permitted to marry as a concession to our weakness.

4) The misuse of sex is strongly condemned. The sexual relation is to express uniquely the total, lasting, binding commitment between a man and a woman.

Greek and oriental thought. As the early Christians moved into all areas of the Roman Empire, they had to struggle for survival—not only their lives but also their basic convictions were at stake. One major area of tension was the clash between the Hebrew-Christian view of man, including his sexuality, and the dualism of Greek and oriental thought. In this battle the positive biblical view of sexuality was lost.

David Mace states it thus. The religious views of the Orient were world-denying. The material world was an illusion, the spiritual world reality. Religious seekers renounce the world, the life of the body and particularly the sexual life. This can be illustrated from a statement about the Buddhist attitude toward sexual desire:

> If you are plagued with desire for bodily pleasures, go out to the field where the corpses are burned. As you look at the half-burned bodies and the disjointed bones, you can contemplate the body as it really is. . . . This beautiful girl who stirs me so—what is she really but a bag of skin

filled with a pulp of blood, tissue and repulsive internal organs hung on a grisly skeleton? . . . It is just another body, taking its short and ignoble journey between birth and death, one insignificant swirl of matter in a world full of pain and illusion. Let it go (Mace: 42).

Mace goes on to point out that the attitude of Hinduism is similar. Gandhi reached an agreement with his wife never to have sexual intercourse. Sex was inherently unspiritual, a hindrance to spiritual life.

These views, rooted in oriental thought, came west into the Greek world after Alexander the Great's conquest. In the western world we speak of dualism (Neo-platonism) which pits spirit versus matter, soul versus body, good versus evil. This is in sharp contrast to the Hebrew thought that man is one whole being; body and soul are not separable.

One of the philosophies which stressed this foreign view was Gnosticism which even went so far against that body as to say that Jesus only *seemed* to have a physical body; he didn't really have one. On the basis of this view, the biblical view was distorted: the fall was viewed sexually; the celibacy of John, Jesus and Paul was taken to mean that renunciation of the sexual drive was the only way; and intercourse was actually unholy business (hence, focus on the virgin birth and belief in the immaculate conception of Mary).

If you held the view that the body, including sex, were evil and the spirit was good, you could come out in either of two ways:

1) You could argue, as some new Christians in Corinth did, that just as food is for the stomach and the stomach for food, so the body is for sex and sex is for the body. Therefore do what you feel like doing with your body. It's all bad anyway and your spirit will not be affected by what you do with your body.

2) You could argue that, since the body is evil, you should subdue it, deny its drives, develop your spirit and become a celibate (monk or nun).

The early church. Rooted in this general attitude, the church had a peculiar view of womanhood. "On the one hand, non-sexual, virgin woman was endowed with all spiritual graces and elevated to the high eminence of the Queen of Heaven. On the other hand, sexual woman was viewed as highly dangerous, representing the Gate of Hell" (Mace: 54).

One of the church fathers, Tertullian (150–230) spoke to Christian women in the following way: "Do you know that you are each an Eve? The sentence of God on this sex of yours lives in this age. . . . You are the devil's gateway; you are the unsealer of that forbidden tree. . . . You destroyed so easily God's image, man" (Mace: 54–55).

But the one man whose non-biblical view of sexuality held sway in the church for at least a thousand years is Augustine (354–430). He taught that all expression of sexual desire is unavoidably sinful. Sex in marriage is justified only for procreation. Celibacy is ideal. Marriage is less spiritual. This view was built into the fabric of Western culture and reaffirmed at the Council of Trent (1545–1583). Sexual pleasure is not compatible with the spiritual life.

The Reformation: Luther, Calvin and the Puritans. Martin Luther challenged Roman teaching, including celibacy, but he continued to hold some views of the church which he left. For example, he taught that "the sex life of married people is not pleasing to God," but "God winks at it." John Calvin viewed marriage as second rate, "out of necessity." No really positive view on sexuality emerged out of the Reformation.

The Puritans, both in England and America, were suspicious of anything pleasurable or beautiful. So, across the whole spectrum of the church, we get the impression that Christianity is anti-sexual. William Cole says, "The church has been guilty of preserving and preaching a point of view . . . which is not only unbiblical but also anti-biblical." This may well mean that at least some, if not most, of the negative attitude we ascribe to the church is really a reaction against the church's distortion of the biblical view.

The sexual revolution. In a relatively short span of years we have seen the pendulum swing from a "conspiracy of silence" to "unashamed openness." What were some factors in this radical shift? Human sexuality was studied by science; individuals rejected the dogmas of the church in an assertion of personal freedom; century-old taboos lost their grip on the people; and mass media, literature and movies went as far as they were permitted.

By now we are at the point of being "the sex-saturated society." We no longer have the option of wishing for a society with uniform moral standards; we must accept the fact that we are in a pluralistic setting. We cannot realistically beg, "Stop the world. I want to get off and seek escape." But we should not simply succumb to and give in to the pressures around us. The Christian church has had too much backbone and courage for that. In the past the faith challenged the majority opinion of its surroundings. We need not abdicate that position now.

Some things we will need to accept: that there will be a wide range of attitudes and acts in our society; that we will continue to be bombarded openly by relentless sexual stimuli; that the church will not be able to resort to compulsion in order to enforce morality.

Some aspects of the sexual revolution will need to be recognized as negative:

1) There is needless suffering, especially among the young who engage in premature experimentation: unwanted pregnancies, abortions, forced marriages, venereal diseases. And yet it is impossible to predict the long-range psychological and spiritual suffering that will result.

2) The flood of pornography has a twisting and distorting effect on person's understanding of sexuality. The photography may be excellent but the view of sexuality is very superficial.

3) The new era of permissiveness has not lived up to its promises that if only we were free we would achieve utopia. Free sex is not salvation.

4) The comparative indifference with which even Christians treat marital infidelity, breakdown and failure is disheartening. We need to ask again where we have placed our values.

The church ought to speak to one other aspect in our situation. Amidst all of the openness a search is going on—a search for meaning. In spite of all the bravado mustered by people there is deep-seated confusion. Here our faith must do some thorough work.

Values. Mace suggests that Christians must decide, "What are the values we cherish for human beings?" Values include justice, respect for persons, integrity, compassion, consideration, trust, love and commitment. Are these the things we hold high (or do we value infidelity, lust, exploitation of another person)? If we value the former, the best way of expressing these values is through monogamous, permanent, binding marriages.

This view is not a reversal to those held "before the revolution." Rather, it is a rediscovery of the profound view of sexuality found in the Bible. The revolution has corrected the distortion that sex is defilement. We wholeheartedly accept the view that the sexual life of married persons can be for them a source of spiritual, personal enrichment.

In conclusion we need to admit our confusion; we need to decide on values; we need to teach our values to each other and our children; and we must trust that they will use their freedom responsibly.

To help us examine the many issues it may be in order to use Jesus' words and apply them rigorously. "Treat other people exactly as you would like to be treated by them—this is the essence of all true religion" (Matthew 7:12, Phillips).

23

FAMILY LIFE: REMINDERS, HABITS, HOPES

Hear, O Israel: The Lord is our God, the Lord alone. You shall love the Lord your God with all your heart, and with all your soul, and with all your might. Keep these words that I am commanding you today in your heart. Recite them to your children and talk about them when you are at home and when you are away, when you lie down and when you rise. Bind them as a sign on your hand, fix them as an emblem on your forehead, and write them on the doorposts of your house and on your gates. . . . When your children ask you in time to come, "What is the meaning of the decrees and the statutes and the ordinances that the Lord our God has commanded you?" then you shall say to your children, "We were Pharaoh's slaves in Egypt, but the Lord brought us out of Egypt with a mighty hand. The Lord displayed before our eyes great and awesome signs and wonders against Egypt, against Pharaoh and all his household. He brought us out from there in order to bring us in, to give us the land that he promised on oath to our ancestors. Then the Lord commanded us to observe all these statutes, to fear the Lord our God, for our lasting good, so as to keep us alive, as is now the case. If we diligently observe this entire commandment before the Lord our God, as he has commanded us, we will be in the right" (Deuteronomy 6:4–9, 20–25).

Train children in the right way, and when old, they will not stray (Proverbs 22:6).

We have this treasure in clay jars, so that it may be made clear that this extraordinary power belongs to God and does not come from us. We are afflicted in every way, but not crushed; perplexed, but not driven to despair; persecuted, but not forsaken; struck down, but not destroyed (2 Corinthians 4:7–9).

This year was named by the United Nations as the International Year

---

First preached in November 1994 at Bethel Mennonite Church, Langley, British Columbia.

of the Family. In connection with that theme, many books, articles and studies have been written about the experience of people in families. Sometimes the emphasis has been on values and the way families used to be; sometimes the emphasis has been on the widespread cancer of abuse: parents of children, brothers and sisters of each other, uncles and relatives in relation to children and teens. Isaac Block did a study of Mennonite church families in Winnipeg and found startling and discouraging evidence that abuse was not at all missing from our families. It was there as it is in the rest of society. We have read and listened very carefully because this is stuff that we know about, if not personally, then via the media or through friends and relatives.

During this year of the family we have also been reminded that even in our relatively strong families, there is tension, sometimes shouting, slamming, swearing, avoidance, irresponsibility, adultery, separation, divorce and common-law living. These things happen among Christians. One of the great problems and tensions in our time is that we believers have high ideals and expectations, a very high view of marriage and family life, yet we fail to live up to our own norms.

I do not want to sweep any of these realities under the carpet, pretending they are not there, nor do I want to continue to name the giants in our culture against whom we are competing. I will mention several other things that we deal with in our families, but we also want to focus on some of the strengths, the potential for good that there is in our families. We will not ignore the dark side, but we also want to light a few candles, candles of hope and faith and optimism. I want to speak about reminders and habits and hopes. These are all intertwined. I expect that each of us will be busy within our own minds and hearts processing, digesting, remembering, arguing, wondering . . .

Let's first consider the texts. Two of them are definitely focussed on the family while one is not. The passage from Deuteronomy serves to remind us as parents and grandparents that we are to be tone-setters within our homes. We as adults are challenged first to love the Lord our God with heart and soul and mind and strength. We are challenged to model a life of faith for the younger generation and we are challenged to speak words of faith to the children. We need the larger circle of the church to help us get the story straight.

The second passage, "Train children in the right way, and when old, they will not stray," is also familiar. What a promise! What a challenge! What confident assumptions! Do things right and everything will turn out right. You may already have been thinking, "Get real, man, you're out of touch;" or, "Yes, but. . . . we tried to do things right but not everything turned out right." That's the way it is in our family and I suspect in most of yours. We know of many situations where the confidence of this verse has been shattered. And yet we cling to it, we must, but realistically.

Paul's word to the Corinthians is not about family; it's about himself and other ministers and the church. But I want to use it for the family. "We have this treasure in earthen jars." The clay jar suggests earthiness, fragility, the possibility of being shattered. The vessel which carries the treasure is faulty. As a carrier of the gospel, Paul knew he was a flawed vessel. As carriers of family values, faith, commitment and parenting, all treasured things, we with Paul would have to admit that we are imperfect vessels. We too, like the clay pot, are fragile, vulnerable.

The fragile nature of Paul's life as a vessel is described in very powerful language: "hard pressed on every side, but not crushed; perplexed but not driven to despair, . . . struck down but not destroyed" (2 Corinthians 4:8–9). What a loaded set of phrases. Think how appropriate these words are for our family experiences. Think of hard pressed, perplexed, struck down, not crushed, not despairing, not destroyed in relation to family. Each of us could unpack this with "for instance" after "for instance:" our relationships as spouses, as parents to children, in relation to our own parents, the relationship between brothers and sisters in the family.

To paraphrase Richard Neuhaus, every family has "its contradictions and compromises, its circus of superficiality, and its moments of splendour;" or as Henri Nouwen says, "pleasantries of life as well as gaping wounds." Yes, moments of splendour, of ecstacy, of good communication, of understanding, of forgiveness—if it weren't for them we might well feel like we were being crushed and driven right out of our minds.

Proverbs reminds us of the potential; Paul reminds us both of the contradictions as well as the promise, the treasure. Let our hope take root in the fact that our faith can be lived and shared in our homes, but no one can give another person faith. Our efforts, no matter how good they are, do not guarantee that our youth will walk the disciple path that we have tried to show them.

We need to be reminded that we face strong opposition. There is much in our culture which is anti-family, anti the values and the faith we hold. In addition to the stuff that happens between us in our own family circles—angry words, terrifying silences, anxiety, fear, pain, impatient waiting, rebellion, walking out and slamming doors—there is the larger world of secularism: to live as though God did not matter;

individualism which is counter to our striving to be a family and church; materialism which stresses possessions out of all proportion to their worth; and a pulse beat which has been labelled as power, entertainment, pleasure, sex and peer pressures.

How can we help each other in these matters? Why not learn to lean the way people in the church were intended to lean: on each other, being vulnerable, self-disclosing, breaking the silence of pretending that all is well when we know we are in trouble and pain and are having a terrible time coping. The family circle is too small. We need the wider perspective of the family of faith which is formed and informed by the Jesus story.

Norman Cousins, former editor of *Saturday Review,* writes, "Can one man [family] do anything? One family cannot do everything but one thing that can be done is to connect our convictions with the convictions of others. You get a multiplying power as you connect." Let's connect and name the problems, the opposition; let's connect and name the resources we've found helpful; let's connect and help each other develop hopeful habits—that is the value of the community of faith.

The habits that allow faith and commitment and trust in God to emerge are: worship, reading, reflection, prayer, consistent living and relationships. Faith-forming, faith-nurturing habits have a cumulative impact on our day-to-day relationships with spouses, children, siblings. Hopeful habits lead to a transformation of life and a consistent devotion to others in our families. Do we advocate our faith by habits of nearness—being involved in church, rituals, stories, friendships—as well as by habits of directness—encouraging exploration in open-ended ways, inviting them to respond from the heart?

From the family of faith we are reminded of an underlying word about how we live with each other. Paul wrote to the Thessalonians, "We were gentle among you, like a nurse tenderly caring for her own children" (1 Thessalonians 2:7). I wonder whether this may not be one of the key roles of the church in our families: that through our Christian fellowship we are reminded of the story that shapes us and gives us the basics of our faith: what we believe about God, God's relation to the world, how we may connect with God, the importance of life in the body, and the reminder one to another that in all of our teaching, exampling and modelling, we are to be gentle, gentle as a nurse—one who responds to the needs of the patient, not imposing her own agenda but always responding appropriately. We are to teach and discipline and evangelize gently, in a winsome way. Developing habits of Christian living may tip the balance in the direction of fulfilling our hopes and dreams. But habits, no matter how good, will not guarantee success.

Let us commit our efforts to God in trust, as though our efforts were nothing; but also spare no effort in doing all we can to facilitate healthy, hopeful relationships. When all is said and done we will need to be patient and wait, sometimes suffering and grieving, sometimes waiting and grieving, hoping that what we have done will be blessed by the Lord and will bear fruit.

24

THE DAVID IN US ALL

*In the spring of the year, the time when kings go out to battle,
David sent Joab with his officers and all Israel with him; they
ravaged the Ammonites, and besieged Rabbah. But David remained in Jerusalem.*

*It happened, late one afternoon, when David rose from his
couch and was walking about on the roof of the king's house, that
he saw from the roof a woman bathing; the woman was very
beautiful. David sent someone to inquire about the woman. It was
reported, "This is Bathsheba daughter of Liam, the wife of Uriah
the Hittite." So David sent messengers to get her, and she came
to him, and he lay with her. (Now she was purifying herself after
her period.) Then she returned to her house. The woman conceived; and she sent and told David, "I am pregnant."*

*So David sent word to Joab, "Send me Uriah the Hittite." And
Joab sent Uriah to David. When Uriah came to him, David asked
how Joab and the people fared, and how the war was going. Then
David said to Uriah, "Go down to your house, and wash your
feet." Uriah went out of the king's house, and there followed him
a present from the king. But Uriah slept at the entrance of the
king's house with all the servants of his lord, and did not go
down to his house. When they told David, "Uriah did not go
down to his house," David said to Uriah, "You have just come
from a journey. Why did you not go down to your house?" Uriah
said to David, "The ark and Israel and Judah remain in booths;
and my lord Joab and the servants of my lord are camping in the
open field; shall I then go to my house, to eat and to drink, and
to live with my wife? As you live, and as your soul lives, I will not
do such a thing." Then David said to Uriah, "Remain here today,
also, and tomorrow I will send you back." So Uriah remained in
Jerusalem that day. On the next day, David invited him to eat and*

Preached in September 1992 at a chapel service at Canadian Mennonite Bible
College; adapted from a sermon first preached in 1988 at First Mennonite
Church, Winnipeg, Manitoba.

drink in his presence and made him drunk; and in the evening he went out to lie on his couch with the servants of his lord, but he did not go down to his house.

In the morning David wrote a letter to Joab, and sent it by the hand of Uriah. In the letter he wrote, "Set Uriah in the forefront of the hardest fighting, and then draw back from him, so that he may be struck down and die." As Joab was besieging the city, he assigned Uriah to the place where he knew there were valiant warriors. The men of the city came out and fought with Joab; and some of the servants of David among the people fell. Uriah the Hittite was killed as well. . . . When the wife of Uriah heard that her husband was dead, she made lamentation for him. When the mourning was over, David sent and brought her to his house, and she became his wife, and bore him a son (2 Samuel 11:1–17, 26–27).

This text is an interesting but also a sad and disappointing passage which reflects some of the tragic realities of life in relationships. Why is this text not heard in our churches? Is the subject not relevant enough? Or are we generally scared to death to tackle it publicly? Shouldn't the church address these issues? I think it should. Let the biblical understanding of sexuality, commitment and faithfulness be heard.

Certainly it's as current as any movie or soap story. It's about stuff that is reported on in our Mennonite papers. It's related to material every pastor encounters and deals with regularly: marriage, adultery, sexuality, faithfulness, sin, forgiveness, confrontation, temptation, lust, seduction, the use of power and position in relationships, giving in to the sexual advances of a public figure. These are issues which most parents are anxious about. It's something which most, if not all, of us have had our own private concerns and thoughts and struggles with. While our culture and society are in a state of visual and verbal exhibitionism on matters sexual and relational, the church too often has been silent. A Christian, biblical understanding of these things needs to be known and heard.

Some may be wondering why this is being done here at College. There are several reasons. First, we are in a relational greenhouse. Relationships spring up quickly in a close community; there is opportunity to spend time with each other morning, noon and evening. Secondly, for many students this may be the first time that they are some distance from home; they enjoy their coming into adulthood and having a lot of freedom. But some are not mature enough to handle that freedom; some abuse it; some do some pretty stupid and harmful things. Thirdly, relationships develop rapidly, sometimes neurotically, with unhealthy, negative effects. Intentions about doing our best in study evaporates, habits suffer, marks tumble, the circle of friends narrows to the exclusion of others: "I have to spend all my time with you, I love you so much." Finally, some people are too obsessed with the question of choosing a life partner.

I want to use the old story of David and Bathsheba to identify some of the issues we might think about.

The setting. The previous chapter in Samuel depicts an external battle between Israel and the Ammonites. This external battle in which David's forces win is set alongside the internal battle in which David loses. John H. Hayes has observed that "the greatest threats lie not in external forces but in the twisted contours of the heart."

David is at leisure on the rooftop of his home, overlooking other smaller rooftops. He happens to see a woman bathing. In his eyes she's a 10. Then a lustful thought enters his mind. He is aroused by her beauty. His desire drives him to action and the sinning begins. He sends someone to check out who she is and finds out she's married to one of his generals. He could have stopped there but he just couldn't help himself. David knows Uriah is in battle. He takes the next step: sends someone to get the woman. After all, he is the king. He doesn't consider his action as exploitation. And she came to him and he slept with her.

The struggle. The story doesn't say a word about David's struggle, if he struggled at all. Did he think about his wife, his children? What about the seventh commandment, "Do not commit adultery?" Did he think, "I'll just have this afternoon affair and that will be the end of it?" Neither does the story focus on Bathsheba and her struggle. She is pictured as passive. What did she struggle with? Did she simply shift responsibility, "After all, he is the King? How could I refuse?" Wouldn't this encounter be a privilege for her?

The complications. Bathsheba becomes pregnant. David strategizes and thinks of three alternatives. Call Uriah the husband. If he spends a night or two with his wife they'll make love and the birth of the child will be on schedule. Problem solved. Simple. But Uriah won't sleep with his wife. He's a high-minded professional soldier who knows it's against the rules to take a break from battle to have a rendezvous with his wife. In contrast to David he lives up to his standards. Plan B: I'll get this guy drunk and surely he'll stumble into his wife's bed. But even after the party he lives up to the rules and doesn't go home. Plan C:

David signs Uriah's death warrant and sends him into the thick of battle and he is killed. Bathsheba mourns his death and David takes the pregnant widow to become his wife.

End of the matter? No. God is on the edges of this messy picture. "The thing David had done displeased the Lord" (11:27b). The whole situation is of concern to God. Nathan the prophet is sent to remind David of his sin: "You are the man!" (12:7)

David confesses, "I have sinned against the Lord." And Nathan offers forgiveness, "The Lord has put away your sin" (12:13).

Sexuality. David saw, he wanted, he sent for, he slept with her. Is that what sexuality is all about? These two were married, but what about those unmarried? Our society, and even surveys among church members young and old, indicate that many singles feel its quite OK to see, desire and have sexual relations. It's called recro-sex.

Gordon Sinclair, writing in the *Winnipeg Free Press* (December 9, 1982) entitled an article, "Hooray for the End of Sex." He quotes George Leonard who wrote in *Esquire* magazine: "Sex has become mere sport, divorced not only from love and creation, but from empathy, compassion, morality, responsibility, and sometimes even common politeness."

Not too long ago Magic Johnson proclaimed that he was dedicating his remaining time to "preach safe sex." And many agree with him that the key issue is safe sex. Is it? Columnist Anna Quindlen wrote in praise of safe sex, saying that she was far less concerned about her children's lifestyles than their lives. To this James Wall in *Christian Century* replied, "Anna Quindlen is wrong. Lifestyle is life. How we live determines who we are. Mere survival is not sufficient to define a full life. Our religious tradition understands that our sexual conduct is at the heart of who we are."

Another writer says, "A Playboy mentality is now the norm for most people in our society and the rest of us feel pressured toward silent acceptance. Safe sex will not protect teenagers (or adults) from the distortions in their sense of values that sex without fidelity or emotional commitment may invisibly inflict upon them."

Is sexuality a mere compartment of our lives or are we at the core body-persons? My being a male defines me as a person; your being female defines you as a person. Our sexuality is the form we take in life as persons. And there are significant differences between female sexuality and male sexuality which we ought to know about and understand. Or can we flippantly say, "Oh, it's only sex." Sexuality involves who we are before God, in our own eyes and in relationship with others. Sexuality is fascinating, deeply mysterious, scary and a powerful dimension of life. It's at the centre of who we are as persons. It is who we are before it is what we do.

Power, exploitation and pressure. David was the one with power and position and he used it fully. "The king wants you. Come lie with me." This raises the questions of males dominating females in many male-female relationships. It touches on the question of date-rape, of pretending to love: "I love you so much, I can't help myself." "If you loved me you would . . . . " "I need you so much. . . ."

On the other hand, "If you loved me you wouldn't be pressuring me!"

Love. There are several types of love. There's *object-centred love*, in which the other is simply used, has no personhood. There's *projective love* which centres on the other's virtues and qualities. They are exaggerated; all blemishes are ignored. This is merely infatuation. There's *conscious love* in which the other is seen as they are, warts and all, where commitment is an open-eyed decision. Then there's *agapeic love* which is other-centred and unconditional.

We've touched on a few of the issues we face. We need to talk about these matters because the good news of the gospel is for the whole person. In the Sermon on the Mount, where Jesus deals with a number of gutsy issues, he also deals with lust and adultery. Our profession to follow Christ as Lord and Saviour includes our sexuality. Our Christian faith gives us a perspective on all of our lives; it informs our attitudes; it shapes our values; it points to life's priorities. We are united to Christ by faith as body-persons. We are called to live as disciples on the slippery slopes of life, intellectually, relationally and sexually. If Jesus is Lord of all, he is Lord of our being sexual persons.

25

FACING UP TO AGING

Just over a year ago, I celebrated my 60th birthday. Already prior to that I became aware that for some unknown reason some waitresses assumed I was a senior. It was at Arby's. "Would you like to have a senior's card?" I got one, and it gives me 10 percent off every meal I buy at Arby's. We also order from the senior's menu in restaurants—it's both cheaper and the amount of food meets our needs better.

Aging and adolescence. So what does it feel like to be getting older, to be called a senior? I suppose this stage in life is just as individual as one of the earlier stages, adolescence. Each person experiences it in their own peculiar way. Adolescence is *Sturm und Drang*—storm and stress: increased independence, important decisions regarding faith, life partner, vocation, where to live, identity and how to manage money matters on one's own. When we were teens we all pretended to be "with it," to know what was going on, to have the answers to the questions we faced.

Getting older is sort of the reverse of adolescence. It also involves considerable storm and stress. But now it is not increasing independence but a return to greater dependence after having had decades of self-sufficient life behind us. *Sturm und Drang?* You bet, but we usually put on a brave front and pretend that, just as we have managed life till now, we will manage getting older. Often we are unwilling or unable to admit, even to ourselves, that we are not always on top of things, that we are subject to new kinds of pressures and stresses.

Getting older is part of the adult life cycle. Psychiatrist Erik Eriksson spoke of the eight stages of human life with the last three covering adulthood. Each period has its primary task: young adulthood: intimacy versus isolation; middle adulthood: generativity versus self-absorption; older adulthood: integrity versus disgust. Aging is a time of significant transition: less money, more time for second career or service or recreation; change in living arrangements. Getting older has implications in several areas.

First preached in November 1994 at Bethel Mennonite Church, Langley, British Columbia.

Theological implications. Old age is an intrinsic part of human life before death. Sometimes these days are called evil and are not enjoyable (Ecclesiastes 12:1). Aging means more than fear, infirmity and death. It touches all the large questions: What is the meaning of my life? Who am I apart from my work? Has my life been fulfilling in God's eyes? Aging does not bring emptiness; it only increasingly reveals what is or is not there. It does not mark an end, but rather the beginning of making sense of the end questions so that life can have an end in every sense of the word (Ann Belford Ulanov, "Aging: On the Way to One's End," in *Ministry with the Aging,* ed. William M. Clements: 109–123).

Religious participation declines with age but people become more religious as they age. Regarding pastors and the elderly: "Ministers often prefer to serve the younger ones, but cannot treat the elderly as one uniform group. There will be more of them; they will be healthier, fill more work and/or volunteer roles, seek more educational/artistic opportunities, and more will live their lives in natural communities" (Barbara Payne, "Religion and the Elderly in Today's World," in Clements: 153–174).

Sociological implications. Older people are the links between the former and the next generations. What are we and have we been giving to the younger generation? Sometimes we berate the young, but studies by Donald Posterski and Reginald Bibby show that the attitudes displayed by teens are remarkably similar to the attitudes found among their elders.

Psychological implications. Older people are expected to show forth wisdom belonging to the mature years and to admit to themselves and to others, as Joshua and Samuel put it, "I am old" (Joshua 23:2; 1 Samuel 12:2). Aging involves reassessment of life, gaining identity as an older person: "Is or was life meaningful or absurd?" We are hurt by the dominant attitude in our culture which glories in youth, strength, vitality. There is the distinct feeling that the older are being pushed aside with an air of indifference: "Move over, old man, and make room for us."

Aging involves a number of *fears.* Some years ago, Paul Miller my former seminary professor wrote an article entitled, "Fears the aged hesitate to talk about" (*Gospel Herald,* January 27, 1981):
   – fear that memory loss may signal senility even while joking about loss of memory;
   – fear that the wisdom accumulated over the decades will be deemed outdated and replaced;
   – fear that society regards them as worse off than they really are;

– fear of forced changes like loss of heirlooms, owning a house, driving, and they don't show much anger because they grew up when it was considered unchristian to express anger;

– fear loss of autonomy and self-direction;

– fear people around them will tire of repeated stories of loss and resultant grief;

– fear of relentless inflation and the possibility that they will need to become dependent on others;

– fear of being left alone since children live far away;

– fear leisure, not working after having lived the work ethic;

– fear looking in the mirror while aware that society prizes smooth skin and vitality and they have wrinkles and display tiredness;

– fear that their last days might be painful and, should they linger, that they become a burden to loved ones.

Older people spend more time at home, more time alone, more time resting.

Predictable changes will include illness, gradual deterioration of health, inability to manage life themselves. Older people will feel more and more helpless, sometimes confused. They wonder: How do they relate to their grown sons and daughters and grandchildren? Will they adjust to the new situation in a care facility? within the limitations and capacities of their physical and mental health?

Response to **Sturm und Drang,** *fears and changes.* First, older people need a community in which they feel connected, a community which cherishes the faith and values they claimed earlier. Church can be a community of caring. How is care made practical and visible? What can we do to allow for and promote inclusion rather than isolation?

Secondly, they need a community that advocates for them and seeks justice by law. "Law is God's way of getting his will done in spite of our unwillingness to do it freely and without coercion" (Martin Heinecken: 86). Church must join with others of good will to advocate justice for the elderly by means of just laws justly enforced.

Even in nursing homes we must be vigilant regarding the conditions. For example, are the elderly being overly drugged and sedated so that they remain quiet? Anne's grandmother lived to be 110. Some years ago medication was reduced to a minimum and we all realized that she was not a zombie. She was alert, had a strong voice and had a will. She was more difficult for the staff to handle but she was certainly more alive. Or, note the 96-year-old who was tied to the hospital chair, completely tired out, but she was there because someone decided it was good for her to be up. Good? by whose decision? Can't a 96-year-old lie in bed if she feels like it? Or at least be in a chair for shorter, less tiring periods? What about elderly who are still in their own homes or apartments? Who looks in on them every morning and later in the day?

Thirdly, they need to practice memory and worship, the inner quest for meaning and wisdom. Seniors must be included, integrated and valued in the worship life of the church. This may mean acceptance by the younger people, listening to their pilgrimage of faith, worship and service, singing their songs.

Fourthly, they need to deal with their own mortality and the loss of friends and loved ones, including spouse. Aging is an inevitable yet proper phase of life. Abraham was referred to as "an old man, full of years, and was gathered to his people" (Genesis 25:8).

Yet they must be realistic. Ecclesiastes refers to the time after youth as "evil days" (12:1) in which they have "no pleasure." There is no pleasure in being fearful of being forsaken when their "strength is spent" (Psalm 71:9), no pleasure in fading eyesight (Genesis 48:10). "Can I discern what is pleasant and what is not? Can your servant taste what he eats or what he drinks? Can I still listen to the voice of singing men and singing women?" (2 Samuel 19:35).

Times are different in our urban setting. In the rural era, retirement was never an issue. There was always something to do on the farm; there was intergenerational involvement. The church must help the elderly cope with repeated experiences of grief, illness, loneliness, the feelings of uselessness and the questions of death and dying. It must provide support, insight, skills, leadership, frequent visits and audio tapes of worship services.

"God, grant me the serenity to accept the things I cannot change; courage to change the things I can; and wisdom to know the difference."

Lord, you have been our dwelling place in all generations. Before the mountains were brought forth, or ever you had formed the earth and the world, from everlasting to everlasting you are God. You turn us back to dust, and say, "Turn back, you mortals." For a thousand years in your sight are like yesterday when it is past, or like a watch in the night. . . . For all our days pass away under your wrath; our years come to an end like a sigh. The days of our life are seventy years, or perhaps eighty, if we are strong; even then their span is only toil and trouble; they are soon gone, and we fly away. . . . So teach us to count our days that we may gain a wise heart (Psalm 90:1–4, 9–10, 12).

Christian
Living

26

CHASING AFTER WIND

As he was setting out on a journey, a man ran up and knelt before him, and asked him, "Good Teacher, what must I do to inherit eternal life?" Jesus said to him, "Why do you call me good? No one is good but God alone. You know the commandments: 'You shall not murder; You shall not commit adultery; You shall not steal; You shall not bear false witness; You shall not defraud; Honor your father mother.'" And he said to him, "Teacher, I have kept all these since my youth." Jesus, looking at him, loved him and said, "You lack one thing; go, sell what you own, and give the money to the poor, and you will have treasure in heaven; then come, follow me." When he heard this, he was shocked, and went away grieving for he had many possessions (Mark 10: 17–22).

Today I want to preach on what a psychiatrist has called "the mass neurosis of our time," the loss of meaning, the loss of a sense of purpose. The title of this sermon is found in the New English Bible translation of the book of Ecclesiastes. The Revised Standard Version reads, "striving after wind," the King James Version, "vexation of spirit."

The writer of Ecclesiastes is a participant-observer in life, and he really lived it up. The book gives us a summary evaluation of the things he tried. Repeatedly one comes across the expression, "chasing after wind." He tried wisdom, pleasures, wine, possessions, women—anything he jolly well felt like. "Then I turned and reviewed all my handiwork, all my labour and toil, and everything was emptiness and a chasing after wind" (Ecclesiastes 2:11). Sometimes we wish, "If only I had the money I would do this or that." Well, this fellow had the money, he tried it all, and he concluded, " It's a chasing after wind."

In more recent years, Viktor Frankl, Austrian psychiatrist, in his book *Man's Search for Meaning,* writes of his three years in German

---

First preached in October 1970 at First Mennonite Church, Winnipeg, Manitoba.

concentration camps at Ausschwitz, Dachau and others. He tells about a daily ration of 5½-ounce slices of bread and watery soup, working in torn shoes or barefoot in the middle of winter, being worn down to skin and bones, fighting disease, separated from wife and children, never knowing when his number will be called to take the final march to the gas chamber. Frankl lived through and writes about those dreadful years. Many of his fellow inmates saw no meaning in their hardship and suffering and daily hovering on the brink of death. They gave up: "It's a chasing after wind; it's useless. Why not give up and die?" This situation is quite different than the first example, but those caught up in it ask similar questions to those who have no apparent needs.

Most of us aren't in either of these classes: having such an abundance of wealth that we can try whatever enters our minds, or facing the deprivation of a concentration camp. We stand somewhere in the middle, but our lives force us to raise the same questions: "Is our life a 'chasing after wind' or is there some meaning and purpose in it all?" Let's think about these issues together.

A student from Yale University who had tried drugs and LSD later wrote about his reasons for doing so. "Drugs looked like an answer to many bewildering questions I faced. I thought they would tell me who I was and where my life was going" (*Readers Digest* reprint, April 1968). This student concluded, "Drugs are emptiness and a chasing after wind."

Students aren't the only ones searching for meaning. Some North American women are on the prowl. One middle-aged housewife was asked about life's meaning. Her reply: "If you mean, am I busy? Yes, between a full-time job and several family crises in the past few years, my time has been well occupied. If you mean, am I doing anything particularly creative. No, I feel I'm marking time." In her book, *The Feminine Mystique* (1963), Betty Friedan insists that diapers, dust and dishes are not the road to meaning, that the life of the homemaker is essentially unfulfilling. It is emptiness, "a chasing after wind." The more aggressive types among women are now demanding all sorts of equalities in our male-dominated society, apparently hunting for meaning and purpose with a vengeance.

Professional people also search. David Shenk, Mennonite Church missionary in Belgium, tells how he became a colleague of a director of schools in Brussels. He wanted to get to know this man so he arranged for a meeting. Shenk told him that he wanted to get to know him personally. The other replied, "Well, now, that's interesting. You know, people think I'm an atheist, but I think there's got to be something—but how do you gear into it? You know very well that I'm working hard all the time, just keeping busy with activities? Do you know why that is. In order to forget the loneliness and emptiness right in the middle of my being, that's why. If I'm batting myself out in the activities, it's so that I can forget the terrible emptiness of my life." For this educator, his endless activity became "a chasing after wind," an escape from facing up to the questions which life placed in his path.

Some search for meaning; others drown the questions which life places before them. They avoid searching. One person described some of his friends this way: "They are occupied with so many activities that they run from one thing to another like overactive teenagers, never even thinking about the meaning of it all."

Some sense the hollowness within and seek ways to disguise it or to compensate for it. Some become prisoner of the will to power which, in its elementary stages, has been described as the will to money. This is a live option for enterprising, energetic sons and daughters of immigrants. They work long hours, become part of the rat race and leave everything—including wife, family and God—except that which promotes getting ahead.

Others become prisoner of the will to pleasure. They seek satisfaction in sexual gratification, sexual compensation.

Still others become prisoner of the illusion of the laugh. Shenk argues that "much hollowness in the empty west is pierced by the laughter of the professional fool. . . . We spend more money in the empty west for humour, comedians, entertainers than most underdeveloped countries spend on their annual budgets. . . . The laugh is the illusion, the reality, the emptiness, the loneliness, the gnawing solitude that is numbed but not eliminated."

Note the story of our text in Mark about the man who had made it in society (Mark 10:17–22). He had nearly everything but found little meaning in what he had. If he were to ask his question today he might put it this way: "What must I do to find meaning in daily life? How can I get out of this rut where nothing seems to satisfy me? How can I live the kind of life that would be worth living forever?"

Jesus challenged him: "Get rid of the things in the way of personal relationships." He offered him fellowship via commitment: "Come, follow me." He challenged him to find his identity in relation to Jesus Christ. But this man could not break out. He was a prisoner of things. He was shackled by meaninglessness. He could not take the steps which would free him for Christ and for others. He was searching for that which would tie together the loose ends of his life—and all he heard was the deceptively simple answer; "Sell, give, come, follow me."

Most of us may not be prisoners of affluence or materialism. We each have our own unique kinds of prisons. What is the wind you are chasing? Jesus' offer stands, "Break out of your prison. Come, follow me." This path may sound too simple, too exclusive, too narrow, too pretentious. But its invitation is part of the scandal of the gospel. Jesus claimed it; the disciples found it. Jesus gives meaning to life. The Christian faith boldly proclaims that in Christ the wind chasing stops.

We are living in a wind-chasing era: people searching for meaning, framework, direction, purpose. Are we with the searching ones or with those who point in the direction where the wind chasing stops, who point to Christ who offers himself and someone to live for?

27

AS YOU RUN . . . LISTEN FOR THE BEAT

[Read Revelation 4–5]

"If a person does not keep pace with his companions, perhaps it is because he hears a different drummer. Let him step to the music which he hears, however measured or far away." These words of Henry David Thoreau got me thinking about the theme, "running the race," and connecting it with an exciting passage of scripture, Revelation 4–5.

Because he ran the race as a follower of Jesus, the apostle John was shipped off to a penal colony in the Aegean Sea around 95 A.D. He was sent there because the state had determined he was running to a different beat than they liked. He dared to run to the beat of Drummer Jesus rather than Drummer Domitian. Domitian beat his drum as emperor of Rome from 81 A.D.–96 A.D. One of the tunes he repeated and insisted that all run to was: "Caesar is Lord; the emperor is God. You must worship him." John and other Christian believers ran to a different drumbeat: "Jesus is Lord. Be faithful unto death." Because they lived in the presence of Christ, had entered his race and heard a different beat, John was exiled and others were persecuted.

While on the island of Patmos, John continued to hear the beat of Jesus and tried to encourage his companions in the race who lived on the mainland to listen for this beat. As a writer, John knew he could not write openly and directly. When the pressure was on, he like others went under cover, writing so that all who had ears for Jesus' beat would hear, and those who did not, would not. How could he as their exiled leader give encouragement as the believers continued to run the race?

Guided by the spirit of God, John came upon a powerful way of encouraging his brothers and sisters to continue to run their race according to Jesus' beat. What he wrote is found in Revelation 4–5. He used weird language and strange symbols to do two things: confuse the opposition and encourage his companions in the race.

This inspired writer was an artist painting an incredible scene—a vision of God on the throne:

First preached in February 1985 at First Mennonite Church, Winnipeg, Manitoba.

At once I was in the Spirit, and there in heaven stood a throne, with one seated on the throne! And the one seated there looks like jasper and carnelian, and round the throne is a rainbow that looks like an emerald. Around the throne are twenty-four thrones, and seated on the throne are twenty-four elders, dressed in white garments, with golden crowns on their heads. Coming from the throne are flashes of lightning, and rumblings and peals of thunder, and in front of the throne burn seven flaming torches, which are the seven spirits of God; and in front of the throne there is something like a sea of glass, like crystal. Around the throne and on each side of the throne, are four living creatures, full of eyes in front and behind (Revelation 4:2–6).

The throne is mentioned in every chapter in Revelation except 2, 8 and 9. It symbolizes authority. Precious stones point to the unspeakable splendour. The rainbow is a sign of promise and hope after tragedy. The 24 elders are heavenly beings which represent 12 tribes and 12 apostles. Victory is depicted by white garments and crowns. Lightning, voices, thunder are all reminiscent of Mount Sinai and the giving of the Law. The sea of glass symbolizes the distance between humans and God. Four living creatures—lion, ox, man, eagle—represent all creation.

The scene comes alive before our eyes; the action unfolds. The four living creatures never cease to sing, "Holy, holy, holy, is the Lord God Almighty, who was and is and is to come" (4:8b). Domitian in Rome may be mighty, but here is One who is almighty. Domitian came in 81 A.D; the Lord was, and is, and is to come—eternal.

The 24 elders catch the beat of the creatures' song. They fall down before the Lord on the throne, cast their own thrones before him, thereby expressing their loyalty. They recognize that whatever authority they have, it is limited. It comes from God. In contrast, Domitian claims to be God himself. The elders sing: "You are worthy, our Lord and God, to receive glory and honor and power, for you created all things, and by your will they were created, and have their being" (4:11). Then John notices the sealed scroll in the hand of him who sits on the throne. It is sealed like a last will and testament. It is the scroll of destiny, sealed but in the hand of God.

Who is worthy to open the scroll and break its seals? No one. John weeps, for he had been promised he would be shown. It appears to him as though there's little chance of that now. One of the elders speaks to him: "Do not weep. See, the Lion of the tribe of Judah, the root of David, has triumphed. He is able to open the scroll and its seven seals." John looks to see the lion, but sees a lamb: a combination of strength and weakness, of pride and humility; the paradox of apparent defeat but actual victory. The weakness of the cross released the greatest power on earth; it unlocks the mystery held in the hand of God. The lamb that was slain did what we could never do for ourselves.

John takes the scroll from the hand of God. And the chorus of four creatures and 24 elders falls down before the lamb, each holding a harp and a bowl of incense, which is the prayers of the saints. Together they sing a new song:

> You are worthy to take the scroll and to open its seals, for you were slaughtered and by your blood you ransomed for God saints from every tribe and language and people and nation; you have made them to be a kingdom and priests serving our God, and they will reign on earth (5:9–10).

The throne, creatures, elders, surrounded by a host of angels, catch the beat and sing: "Worthy is the Lamb who was slain, to receive power and wealth and wisdom and might and honor and glory and blessing!" (5:12). Finally, every creature in heaven and earth joins in the song: "To him who sits upon the throne and to the Lamb be blessing and honor and glory and might for ever and ever!" (5:13). And what did the four creature say? "Amen!" So be it.

In the face of the claim of the emperor, Christians were reminded that men and women meet God in Christ and that the worship of God is free, not forced. The exile on Patmos has appealed to John's fellow believers' imagination and faith. He doesn't threaten them if they should worship Domitian. He paints a picture on a huge canvas and presents them with a crescendo of song which invites them to listen for the beat and run to the beat of a different drummer. By giving them a fresh vision of Christ, the lion-like lamb, he appeals to them to be loyal unto death. He encourages them by showing them creation at worship; he asks them to be ready to die for him who has already died: "Don't give your loyalty and your praise to that puny, arrogant Domitian; give it to him who is creator, ruler, redeemer and Lord. Hear the beat? Run with it and, if need be, die for it!"

Our situation is vastly different than that of John and his brothers and sisters in Asia Minor—and yet it is the same. We are not hearing the drumbeat of Domitian, but we do hear others—beats which are out of harmony, out of step with the beat of Drummer Jesus. Like the Christians of century one, we in 1985 are those who have decided to enter a race—and run it with Jesus as our drummer.

Whether we have been running the race with Jesus for 40 years or for four months, we are called to look at Jesus; we are called to listen for the beat that Drummer Jesus beats and run the race faithfully. That is a call for all Christians. And it's easier to issue this challenge than to do it—because our ears and our hearts hear other beats as well.

As we run the race, we hear the drumbeat of *conformity* which invites us to fit in, to believe and to behave as the average person on the street. The exile on Patmos calls young and old to listen for the beat that Jesus beats. Conformity to the world around us is not worthy of your devotion. Run to the beat of Jesus, and don't let the world squeeze you into its mould.

As we run the race, we hear the drumbeat of *change* which insists that only the recent, newest fads are worth marching to. Change says that the tested and proven ways of the past are not worthy of the person who is really running "with it." To this the exile of Patmos would say; "Don't worship the new and the changing. Give your all to him who was and who is and who is to come. Run to the beat of him who lasts, and examine the new."

As we run the race, we hear the drumbeat of *freedom* which says, "No one will tell me what to do. I can do what I feel like doing. I will not be restricted by convictions, self-control or discipline." To this the exile on Patmos says, "Don't run with the beat of freedom. Remember that only they who submit to the Lord God know true freedom. Running to the beat of Jesus means submission and freedom without limits."

As we run the race, we also hear the drumbeat of *the state* which asks for total, unthinking, uncritical allegiance of all its citizens, even the lives of its young people. To this the exile of Patmos says, "Beware of the drumbeat of the state. Be subject to the state, but don't give it your highest devotion. Running to the beat of Jesus includes calling the powers-that-be to accountability and being subject, but not silent!"

As we run the race, we also hear the drumbeat of *materialism* which invites us to have and to want more and more things, and asks us to measure others and ourselves by what we have. To this beat the exile of Patmos says, "Don't run according to this beat. Running the race with Jesus means placing material values lower on that ladder than the spiritual. That which is done for others in love and for the Lord is of lasting worth."

Do you hear the drumbeats of our time or of eternity? Everyone runs according to some beat. Let us who have decided to run the race with Jesus distinguish between the beats. Let us run to the beat of him whose beat goes on forever and ever. He alone is worthy of our highest devotion.

28

COMMUNITY AND CONFRONTATION

So those who welcomed his message were baptized, and that day about three thousand persons were added. They devoted themselves to the apostles' teaching and fellowship, to the breaking of bread and the prayers (Acts 2:41–42).

One day Peter and John were going up to the temple at the hour of prayer, at three o'clock in the afternoon. And a man lame from birth was being carried in. People would lay him daily at the gate of the temple called the Beautiful Gate so that he could ask for alms from those entering the temple. When he saw Peter and John about to go into the temple, he asked them for alms. Peter looked intently at him, as did John, and said. "Look at us." And he fixed his attention on them, expecting to receive something from them. But Peter said, "I have no silver or gold, but what I have I give you; in the name of Jesus Christ of Nazareth, stand up and walk." And he took him by the right hand and raised him up; and immediately his feet and ankles were made strong. Jumping up, he stood and began to walk, and he entered the temple with them, walking and leaping and praising God. All the people saw him walking and praising God, and they recognized him as the one who used to sit and ask for alms at the Beautiful Gate of the temple; and they were filled with wonder and amazement at what hat happened to him (Acts 3:1–10).

These texts from Acts give us a glimpse into a group's experience of community. There may well be some helpful connections between their experiences and ours as we begin a new year together as a College community.

The group about which these words were written had recently formed and was quite diverse. They had come together around a core group of 120 which had a central group of a dozen. The group had grown by leaps and bounds to over three thousand members. Think

---

First preached in September 1992 at the opening chapel of Canadian Mennonite Bible College's 1992–1993 academic year.

about the problems of orientation and introducing and integrating which they must have faced. They also had to cope with significant obstacles to being a community—barriers of language, culture, previous experiences, and levels of faith and commitment.

What made them a community was their shared bias. At the centre of their experience was a common commitment to the risen Christ and the energizing fiery Spirit that had come upon them in a remarkable way. Because of their shared bias, Jesus and the Spirit, they were utterly enthusiastic with each other. "They devoted themselves to the apostles' teaching and fellowship, to the breaking of bread and the prayers" (2:42).

I was struck by the word "devoted." Questions came to mind: What am I, what are you, really devoted to? What are the things that we can really be enthusiastic about? How will our devotedness stack up against the devotedness of the people in our text? Will it be said of us that we as individuals and as a community of learners will be enthusiastic about biblical teaching, about Christian fellowship, about meaningful table conversation, about prayers?

Those people had a great time in their new community. I would guess that a good many of them would have been tempted to enjoy the in-group cosiness and congeniality, and leave it at that. But that is not what happened. The story that Luke tells indicates that they left the cosy cocoon of their community and became involved in some important confrontations. They ventured beyond the bounds of their community and two of them, Peter and John, were confronted by the lame, crippled man. He was sitting on the temple steps asking for help. They got involved with him, offering to help "in the name of Jesus."

The "cripples" we encounter may not always have visible handicaps but may be lame nevertheless, crippled in private and inner ways which keep them from functioning at full potential. It may be your roommate silently asking for understanding and help; it could be someone sitting on the steps of the pit needing a listening ear and caring heart. The cripples that confront us may be visible and vocal or silent and unseen. Will Peter and John, Sarah and Susan notice those who are crippled in our community?

Another thing: you and I may actually take our turns at being lame and crippled. Our lameness may have to do with our own life story. We may be unsure about our own faith and commitment. We may be uneasy about a crippling lifestyle that we earlier got into. We may be going along from day to day with a secret ailment, abuse, relational problems, frustrations about decisions we need to be making; or about unwise and inappropriate sexual activity we've gotten into; or simply being out of sorts with ourselves, with life and purpose, or with God.

Will we have the courage of the visibly lame to own up to our lameness, our vulnerability, and seek help? Will there be enough Peters and Johns, Susans and Sarahs in our midst who will have hearing ears and perceiving eyes and caring hearts with which to notice the signs of need and of lameness in others?

In addition to being a comfortable and cosy community—affirming and enjoying each other—the question is: Will we also be a community in which personal lameness will be confronted and where healing will be available? We will be concerned about our own relational needs but will we, like Peter and John (or Sarah and Susan), also be open to being interrupted while on our way to something important? Will we be ready to be confronted by the needs of another and be able to offer the healing and restoring word so that someone who is down can be raised and be on the way, walking, leaping and praising God?

In the early stories of Acts, I see another way in which the community experienced confrontation. In fact Luke reports an incident in which the confrontation evoked joyful celebration as well as an incident where the confrontation evoked the deepest pain and disappointment. Both were confrontations within the believing community.

On the one hand, they were joyfully overwhelmed by the generosity and outstanding spirit of one in their midst: Barnabas. You may remember his story. He had a piece of real estate on a nearby island, sold it and brought the proceeds for the benefit of the whole group. We may not have anyone selling real estate and sharing with the rest, but we will have joyful sharing of gifts and talents and experiences. You and I will be confronted by the amazing grace of God at work in the lives of others. As an outgrowth of such confrontation, we will be able to affirm the gifts of others and celebrate with them.

But there was also a very painful kind of confrontation. The community was shocked and pained when the fellowship and commitment to Christ and each other was shattered with deception, half-truth and hypocrisy. Two of their group, Ananias and Sapphira, had fallen into temptation and had become unfaithful. That called for a difficult confrontation; it had to be dealt with head on. I hope we will not see ourselves in the experience of this couple. They were in the cosy, comfortable community but actually they were not in. They felt driven to conceal, to speak half-truth, to act in ways which contradicted the bias of the community.

We could see ourselves in the role of Peter who, in the name of the

Lord and the community and its faith bias, had to deal with those who disregarded the nature of the community of which they were part. The results were extreme: they both dropped dead. I'm not suggesting that we want to deal that way, but I think it is fair to say that we do want to help each other be responsible and accountable as members of this faith-biased community. Peter's role in the matter is to be the community member or leader who is called to confront someone at the point of failure.

By coming to CMBC we have entered a community with a bias, a community in which there will be affirmation, worship and growth in commitment. But this community will also become for us a community of confrontation. We will be confronted by the lameness of others, visible and invisible. We will be challenged to acknowledge our own lameness and seek help rather than deny that we need help. We will be challenged to live with integrity, embodying in our actions, attitudes and words the bias that belongs to being followers of Christ in company with others.

Let us, like the early church, look to God in prayer as we seek to live and serve as we ought.

29

RUDDERS, BITS AND FIRE

Not many of you should become teachers, my brothers and sisters, for you know that we who teach will be judged with greater strictness. For all of us make many mistakes. Anyone who makes no mistakes in speaking is perfect, able to keep the whole body in check with a bridle. If we put bits into the mouths of horses to make them obey us, we guide their whole bodies. Or look at ships: though they are so large that it takes strong winds to drive them, yet they are guided by a very small rudder wherever the will of the pilot directs. So also the tongue is a small member, yet it boasts of great exploits.

How great a forest is set ablaze by a small fire! And the tongue is a fire. The tongue is placed among our members as a world of iniquity; it stains the whole body, sets on fire the cycle of nature, and is itself set on fire by hell. For every species of beast and bird, of reptile and sea creature, can be tamed and has been tamed by the human species, but no one can tame the tongue—a restless evil, full of deadly poison. With it we bless the Lord and Father, and with it we curse those who are made in the likeness of God. from the same mouth come blessing and cursing. My brothers and sisters, this ought not to be so. Does a spring pour forth from the same opening both fresh and brackish water? Can a fig tree, my brothers and sisters, yield olives, or a grapevine figs? No more can salt water yield fresh (James 3:1–12).

When you read the sermon title you may have wondered what this was going to be about, but after you read the text, it became quite clear. Rudders, bits and fire are metaphors used to speak about the mystery and the power of that little member, our tongue. This little member boasts of great things, sometimes great in the dangerous sense, sometimes great in the good sense.

We cannot read these verses without realizing how utterly practical

---

Preached in April 1995 at Peace Mennonite Church, Richmond, British Columbia; adapted from sermons preached on CMBC choir tour, 1992.

James is. This was one of the reasons Luther in the 16th century decided that James wasn't really worth having in the New Testament at all. According to him this was a "right strawy epistle," good for the fireplace. Luther was so overwhelmed by the grace of God which he had experienced that he judged everything else accordingly. Where in James is grace mentioned, or forgiveness, or the love of God? Where is the call to be converted? All these things are absent from James' letter, so Luther concluded it might as well be absent from the New Testament as well.

But we don't agree with Luther's conclusion. We are of the conviction that profession of faith and life ought to be in sync with each other. Our daily life should show that we are children of God seeking to live according to God's will. We are of a practical bent. And we certainly understand James' concern about the tongue. James is so practical that we might even get our toes stepped on.

Speech is mysterious. Words have strange, queer, powerful and sometimes surprising effects. Recall the little ditty we picked up in childhood: "Sticks and stones may break your bones but names will never hurt you." That is a lie! In mysterious and powerful ways, words have the power to hurt or to heal; and when they hurt they hurt deeply; they are inscribed indelibly on our emotional databases and they leave scars for life.

Words carry a lot of freight—and behind the words are feelings and a person. Think for a minute how powerful words are: words inflict pain; they may arouse sorrow, or bring relief. Words express anger and resentment; they may offer support or empathy. They provide joy and stimulate laughter, inflict hurt or resolve conflicts. Words may create barriers, invisible but real barriers which stand longer than the Berlin Wall. They also build bridges of communication and trust and love and hope! Is there anything more important than the use of the tongue?

"Both glory and disgrace come from speaking." In one of the apocryphal books we read, "Many have fallen by the edge of the sword, but not as many as have fallen because of the tongue" (Ecclesiasticus 28:18).

The text in James is intensely practical, but beyond that it has a double focus. On the one hand, "the tongue is a fire, a world of evil among our members; it corrupts the whole person, is itself set on fire by hell, . . . a restless evil, full of deadly poison" (v.6–8).

Can you imagine a more depressing picture? James says the tongue is like a single small spark, which ignites a whole stand of timber, setting ablaze, destroying, practically impossible to extinguish. He goes so far as to say that, although humans have been granted dominion over creatures of the sea, reptiles, birds and animals, and have in fact shown that they can tame and train them, no one can tame the tongue. It is a restless, unruly evil, full of deadly poison. Each of us can recall how words have poisoned the atmosphere and relationships in a family circle, or destroyed a relationship between friends. Proverbs 10:19 says, "When words are many, sin is not absent."

For a long time that is what this passage said to me: the tongue is dangerous, and nothing more. Then, as I immersed myself in this text, the other side caught my attention as well. These other two metaphors, rudders and bits, say something on the flipside. Fire to be sure, but also rudders and bits. What these three have in common is that a comparatively small part—the rudder on an ocean liner, the bit in a large horse's mouth, or the one small spark— all have an influence far beyond their proportionate size. But after that there's a difference. The fire James is talking about is not a cooking fire or a blaze in a fireplace, but a forest fire, damaging, destroying all that is in its path.

The boast of the small rudder and the boast of the bit on the bridle suggest something positive—both are the key to control and direction. The ship is literally controlled and directed by the seemingly insignificant rudder. And the tongue, our tongue, is endowed with a similar capacity—the capacity to control and direct our lives so that life's ship will arrive safely at its destination, no matter what the storms are like. The sleek riding horse, muscular and strong and fast, is controlled and directed by the bit in the horse's mouth. And the tongue, our tongues are endowed with a similar capacity—to control and direct our lives, no matter how fast the pace might be. Now we have the whole picture: the tongue has potential for good or for evil; it can be as destructive as a forest fire, or as helpful as a rudder on a ship.

There is the danger that you and I will use this gift of speech as fire, destroying relationships in family, with friends, in church. We can speak negatively, destructively, to and about others, but we are not compelled to do so. The other possibility is that the tongue is the rudder of our lives and can exercise control and direction, allowing us to reach our God-intended destination. James said, "No mortal can tame the tongue" (v.8). That's true, but the Lord can. At Pentecost the Lord lit another fire which also issued in speech, a fire whose source was not hell, but the Spirit of God. And the tongues of believers were freed to speak good news.

The bit is the means by which the violence of the horse is controlled and the rudder conquers the storm of the sea. What James seems to be saying is that the tongue is the key to controlled living. And the tongue is much more than what we actually express in words: thoughts, feelings, imagination, inclinations all precede the formulation of words.

We use our tongues in positive ways when we use them to express praise to God: in our worship services, and in our devotional times. Think of the positive effect on our lives when we direct our thoughts and our speech to praise God. As James says a little later on, "With our tongues we praise our Lord" (v.9). Praising God gives focus, direction and affects everything else we do.

We use our tongues as rudders and bits when we build bridges of understanding, of trust, of mutual caring. Think what power there is in a word of appreciation, of affirmation, of support.

We use our tongues as rudders and bits when we use speech to create—can we say it that way—laughter; whether that be a smile, a chuckle or uncontrollable, gut-wrenching laughter. In C.S.Lewis' *Tales of Narnia*, we read the passage where Aslan the lion says, "Laugh and fear not creatures. Now that you are no longer dumb and witless you need not always be grave. For jokes as well as justice come in with speech." We humans are laughing creatures. Speech and laughter are uniquely human qualities. Is there a ministry of speech which helps us see the lighter side of things?

The tongue does not have to be a restless evil, full of deadly poison; the tongue does not have to corrupt and spoil our lives. When we use our tongues to express praise to God, to share the good news of salvation with others, to build bridges of trust and understanding, and to help others to laugh, rather than to cry, then the tongue is rudder and bit, not fire. Then it directs our lives in the direction of communion with God and God-intended relationships with others.

Let us resolve to use our tongues more and more as rudders and bits. Let us decide to allow God's spirit to light that fire which issues in worshipful speech, in uplifting and affirming words, in relationships of joy and forgiveness and love.

30

GOD STRENGTHENS

Why do you say, O Jacob, and speak, O Israel, "My way is hidden from the Lord, and my right is disregarded by my God?" Have you not known? Have you not heard? The Lord is the everlasting God, the Creator of the ends of the earth. He does not faint or grow weary; his understanding is unsearchable. He gives power to the faint, and strengthens the powerless. Even youths will faint and be weary, and the young will fall exhausted; but those who wait for the Lord shall renew their strength, they shall mount up with wings like eagles, they shall run and not be weary, they shall walk and not faint (Isaiah 40:27–31).

Before we look at the details of this text, we want to remind ourselves of the situation which gave rise to the complaint or lament of the people with which this text begins.

Context: theirs and ours. The passage opens with questions, three of them, and the opening question signals "lament," complaint about the trap of everyday life, the situation in which they live. Although these words come from a time long past, they resonate with our experience—on two levels. First, on a personal level: Who of us has not turned to this passage or another like it, when we were struggling with that which came our way, whether that be illness, accidents, loss of employment, breakdown of relationships? I think we know what this is about. It's the stuff that we deal with and have to cope with all the time.

Secondly, this passage resonates with our experience as a people. In times past our forebears faced persecution, hardship, refugee experiences, and they were not always sure whether they would come out on top or not. They were threatened, overwhelmed, nearly overcome by the storms of life. And today, we cannot but think of the situation in which we as a church find ourselves—not that we are in a state of exile, not that we are hard pressed by persecution. We are being pressed by affluence, sucked in by materialism and divided by individualism. The

Presented in July 1995 at Wichita '95, the joint sessions of the Mennonite Church and the General Conference Mennonite Church.

situation facing us as a church is one of being overwhelmed by the new situation: rural to urban, separation to assimilation in the culture, plurality of influences on us and our children, new social problems. We feel that the odds are against us. It's quite different than during Isaiah's time but the dynamics are similar.

So what do we do? We struggle, we pray, we complain, we utter the lament, we speak about the changes, the losses, the sense of not being in control of anything anymore. And as we do these things, we realize that we have less energy for that which matters most; we have less vision for the future, and experience an increase of fatigue and hopelessness.

We can well understand the situation of the first hearers of our text. Those people are caught in a situation of exile: the odds were against them; they do not seem to have much of a chance to do anything about it; they hear these words of Isaiah, the prophet of God, from a posture of resignation and a sense of powerlessness, resignation to that which seems formidable and overpowering.

The mood is one of despair, frustration. Brueggemann suggests that this sort of thing has devastating effects on people: "Depressed people do not want to act, and despairing people think it does not matter" (Brueggemann, *Prophetic Imagination*, 73). Further he speaks about an "atheism of despair" which makes the people weary, faint and exhausted.

What we have in our text is the prophet's response to his people caught in this vice grip of despair and hopelessness. What do these despairing, discouraged people need? Do they need a careful analysis of the situation? a survey of attitudes? a prediction of better times to come? Apparently not. Isaiah's approach is different. He addresses their troubling situation "in a shamelessly theological, candidly kerygmatic and naively eschatologically way" (Brueggemann: 9). This is refreshing, is it not?

Isaiah isn't the only one who has responded in this way to people in desperate situations. At the end of the first century in Asia Minor, the Christian church faced incredible odds: Domitian the emperor claiming to be divine, oppression and persecution to the point of martyrdom, hopelessness in the face of insurmountable difficulties. What did the inspired seer John do for those people? John, a prisoner on Patmos, wrote a letter of encouragement to despairing people with their backs to the wall; and, like Isaiah, he did not begin by analyzing the situation, by naming the foe, Rome, nor by suggesting a quick fix for them. Notice what he did in trying to help the people cope with their desperate situation. He too was "shamelessly theological, candidly kerygmatic, naively eschatalogical." He sketched for them a living mural of the Lord and lead them in worship. He was not hurried; he took a lot of time to do this—the first five chapters of Revelation—before describing the details.

What did despairing people in Isaiah's and in John's time need? What did they get? A fresh vision of God, a renewal of vital faith, a new experience of worship. The big question for them was: Will Yahweh get involved in the plight of the people who worship him? Or, is God too high and mighty? Is God remote and distant? Is Yahweh too much concerned about the stars and the nations that he has no energy, no time, no interest in the plight of individual people and of God's people, Israel? Is God willing to be involved?

This is the question which lies beneath the lament in Isaiah 40:27 and leads into our passage. It is the question of justifying God—theodicy it is called. And it gets at the heart of Israel's faith and ours. Is the God whom we worship and serve concerned about us? Does God care? Will the all-powerful God encourage us?

The people's lament. Experience provides the basis for severe testing of faith. The people then and many of us today utter and feel with intensity these words of lament with which our passage begins: "My way is hid from the Lord, and my right is disregarded by my God." When the exiles say, "My way . . .", they are thinking corporately as a people, a people who have been through the wringer of history. For them "the way" has been one of loss, one loss after another, losses piled high. The words of these exiles are similar to words uttered in the Psalms: "Why do you hide your face? Why do you forget our affliction and oppression?" (Psalm 44:24). "Answer me, O Lord. . . . Do not hide your face from your servant, for I am in distress . . ." (Psalm 69: 16a, 17).

The prophet quotes their lament. He is aware of their despair and challenges them with the question: "Why do you say . . . my way is hidden?" The challenge continues with two more questions: "Have you not known? Have you not heard?" (v.28).

What does he mean? How should they have known? Where would they have heard? He may well have based his own convictions on Exodus 3. When the people had been hard pressed as slaves in Egypt, it may have seemed that God had forgotten them, but God was not hiding.

Listen: "I am the God of your father, the God of Abraham, the God of Isaac, and the God of Jacob. . . . I have observed the misery of my people who are in Egypt; I have heard their cry, . . . I know their sufferings" (Exodus 3:6–7). God engaged their memory, the memory of their experiences as a people, and chided them for complaining against God. Their professed faith ought to have given them the perspective with which to cope with the situation, but it needed refreshing.

God challenged his people with a conviction out of their own confession of faith, that "the Lord is the everlasting God, the Creator of the ends of the earth. He does not faint or grow weary; his understanding is unsearchable" (Isaiah 40:28). Coping with difficult realities is enabled by convictions acquired, nurtured earlier in life. It's like someone said, "You don't learn to windsurf in a gale." The God who is everlasting will outlast the present dilemma; the God who is Creator of the ends of the earth will be able to create order out of the utter chaos of their situation. Even though they have grown weary with their daily distress, God is unwearying and will not faint. The all-encompassing understanding of God includes their difficult situation and God knows when help is needed.

In verse 28 we have moved from the immensity of creation to the details of daily reality. Isaiah has linked the greatness of God with the needs of the people: the non-fainting God ministers to fainting creatures; the non-weary God gives life and hope to weary creatures. The picture of God suggested here is that God does not dwell in majestic isolation, is not self-sufficient, is not unmoved by the experiences of the people.

A few chapters further in Isaiah 57:15 our theologian-prophet says: The Lord "dwells in the high and holy place, and also with those who are contrite and humble in spirit." God, the Almighty one, does not only create and control the big picture; God is free, free to act on behalf of the people.

This God does not only create and control the big picture but is also the one who "gives power to the faint, and strengthens the powerless" (v.29). Isaiah's response to the peoples' lament? God is present, God is able, God cares, God is willing. The cloud of hopelessness and the feelings of despair begin to disappear. The word of encouragement sinks deep into their hearts. The promise of help, the promise of power, the renewal of strength comes from God, but there is a human aspect as well.

Waiting is the key. The people are expected to wait . . . what might that mean? Waiting is the alternative to complaining, to uttering the lament, "My way is hidden . . .". Waiting is a challenge to our obsession with having to be active and very busy. Waiting is an act of confident faith, willingness to accept God's authority. Waiting is contrasted with watching current events and asking, "What in the world is going to happen next?" Waiting is not passivity, but actively focussing, giving attention to the presence of the Lord and not only to the realities of the present.

Karl Barth comments on the meaning of this waiting: "It is in receiving and not grasping, in inheriting not possessing, in praising and not seizing." And he goes on to say, "Exiles must always learn that hope is never generated among us but always given to us" (Barth, *Action in Waiting,* 1969).

Waiting is the way to transformation and service. Those who wait thus will have their lives transformed, for the creator God will do for the exiles what he has done for the creation: give life where there is none. New found strength is expressed in soaring, running, walking: "they shall mount up, . . . they shall run, . . . they shall walk" (v.31). Notice the order to these stages: soaring, running and walking. The imagination, the dreaming, the envisioning come first and are the easiest; walking, the daily grind, the actual work of getting the vision implemented is the most difficult. For all of these stages the source of strength is in God.

It is the prophet's role to keep alive the ministry of imagination (Brueggemann: 45). The prophet has found a way—in the midst of grief, despair and fear—to speak a word of hope. He does not deny the reality of their situation. Israel was in fact in captivity; much had been lost: land, temple, king and, above all, hope.

Hope for the people. Hope flies in the face of facts and refuses to accept the reading of reality by majority opinion. The prophetic word offers the people an alternative reading of reality, another way of seeing things, a way not controlled by the outwardly powerful, the political or economic systems, but by the reality of God at work in their lives. And the immobilized people begin to face the future. "The hardware will not immediately surrender and the great kings will not readily surrender" (Brueggemann: 77).

Think of another situation: the situation in which Paul and Silas found themselves when they were imprisoned and in stocks in the Philippian jail. Nothing around them suggested hope, yet at midnight the silence of the prison was interrupted with singing. Yes, singing. Those two believers declared their faith and voiced their hope in spite of the counter-indicators all around them. Isaiah was also one who encouraged imprisoned people, exiled people, people caught in the web of circumstances by singing.

Let's close with this thought: the church, we today, are to take the place of Isaiah, of Paul and of Silas and speak the words of encouragement so that faith can blossom and hope can flourish. We do that because we have faith in Yahweh, the encouraging God.